Women in America

FROM COLONIAL TIMES TO THE 20TH CENTURY

Women in America

FROM COLONIAL TIMES TO THE 20TH CENTURY

Advisory Editors
LEON STEIN
ANNETTE K. BAXTER

A Note About This Volume

Perhaps more than any other form of communication, letters can reveal intimate hopes, sentiments, fears, hesitations, resolves. This collection of letters written by a sensitive woman covers a dozen years of her short life. It begins with a letter to her mother, written in 1797 while she was at boarding school; the last, dated 1809, was set down shortly before her death. In between are the letters reflecting her thoughts and worries, the experiences that made her happy or sad, her longings and her fulfillments. The letters trace her growth, her departure from parents, her marriage and motherhood. Throughout there is fresh spirit, wonder, intelligence and foreboding.

A GIRL'S LIFE EIGHTY YEARS AGO

ELIZA SOUTHGATE BOWNE

ARNO PRESS
A New York Times Company
NEW YORK – 1974

Reprint Edition 1974 by Arno Press Inc.

Reprinted from a copy in
   The University of Illinois Library

WOMEN IN AMERICA
From Colonial Times to the 20th Century
ISBN for complete set: 0-405-06070-X
See last pages of this volume for titles.

Manufactured in the United States of America

Library of Congress Cataloging in Publication Data

Bowne, Eliza Southgate, 1783-1809.
   A girl's life eighty years ago.

   (Women in America: from colonial times to the 20th
century)
   Reprint of the ed. published by Scribner, New York.
   1. United States--Social life and customs--1783-1865.
2. Bowne, Eliza Southgate, 1783-1809. I. Title.
II. Series.
E164.B78 1974   917.4'03'30924 [B]   74-3933
ISBN 0-405-06079-3

A GIRL'S LIFE EIGHTY
YEARS AGO

MRS. WALTER BOWNE.

Miniature by Malbone.

ARTOTYPE, E. BIERSTADT, N. Y.

A GIRL'S LIFE EIGHTY YEARS AGO

SELECTIONS FROM THE LETTERS OF
ELIZA SOUTHGATE BOWNE

WITH AN INTRODUCTION BY
CLARENCE COOK

ILLUSTRATED WITH PORTRAITS AND VIEWS

NEW YORK
CHARLES SCRIBNER'S SONS
1887

The Riverside Press, Cambridge :
Electrotyped and Printed by H. O. Houghton & Co.

INTRODUCTION.

ELIZA SOUTHGATE, the writer of the letters here collected, was the daughter of Robert and Mary Southgate, and was born in Scarborough, Me., September 24, 1783. She was the third in a family of twelve children. Her father came of English stock, and was born in Leicester, Mass., where his family had long been settled. Here he studied medicine, and when he had finished his course he left his native place, where there appeared to be no room for another practitioner, and settled in Scarborough. We are told that, after the primitive fashion of the time, he set out to seek his fortune on horseback, with all his worldly goods in a pair of saddle-bags. In this way he entered Scarborough, where his character and talents were not long in getting him a good position. He had picked up some law, and in a new and small community was able to make his knowledge useful, so that in course of time he was appointed a Judge in the Court of Common Pleas.

He had not been long in Scarborough before he married Mary, the daughter of Richard King, a large landholder in the District of Maine. " Pretty Polly King," as Mary was familiarly called by her friends, was the second daughter of Mr. King by his first wife. The eldest child by this marriage was Rufus—well known for the distinguished part he played in the early history of our country. A third child, Pauline, married Mr. Porter ; their son Moses, whose name often occurs in these letters, was a young man of great promise. He engaged his cousin Eliza in a correspondence, after the somewhat formal fashion of the time ; only her letters remain to indicate its character, but they are among her best. In her lively tilting on the well-worn subject of the education of the sexes, the lady shows herself a clever mistress of the foils, and there are not wanting indications that the combatants did not escape from the encounter heart-whole. But however this may have been, all was ended by the sudden death of Mr. Porter from a fever caught in boarding an infected vessel in the transaction of some necessary business.

Scarborough was not a large town, but its position as a seaport gave it some importance, and the society was far above what is ordinarily met with in such places. The Hunnewells, Bragdons, Bacons, Emersons, Wadsworths, names that are distinguished in the social history of New England, belong to the early settlers of the neighborhood, and are still represented there. Zilpah, one of the daughters of General Peleg Wadsworth, who are frequently mentioned in these letters, married Stephen Longfellow, a cousin of Mrs. Southgate, and became the mother of the poet, Henry Wadsworth Longfellow.

The Southgates gave their children the best education to be had in those times. They were first sent to school in Scarborough; but, later, were placed—to be " finished," as the old phrase was—at boarding-schools near Boston. When she was fourteen years old, Eliza was sent to a school at Medford, and a letter written from that place gives a rather uncomfortable notion of her surroundings. In these few childish lines, however, the character of the woman is plainly prefigured—her observation, her power of clear, terse statement, her playful humor, her cheerful submission to duty, and her affection for her parents, making her willing to put up with whatever was disagreeable rather than give them uneasiness. However, Dr. Southgate, as a physician, could see that a school where the pupils slept, four beds in a small chamber and two in a bed, was not the place for a growing girl, and he therefore took his daughter away and put her at the school at Medford, kept by Mrs. Rowson. This, for its time, was an excellent school, and Miss Southgate remained there until the day came when " studies" were to be thrown aside, and " life" was to begin. She seems by her letters to have been very happy while under Mrs. Rowson's care—the varied and somewhat romantic life led by that lady perhaps fitted her, better than would have been thought, to be the guide and friend of a girl of Eliza Southgate's peculiar character.*

Her life after she left school is so fully described in her letters that there is no need of following it in detail. She tells her own story far better than another could do it, and much that would inevitably be dull and commonplace narrated in plain prose, sparkles with life under the swift pen of this lively girl. She tells of her visit to Saratoga, with her friends Mr. and Mrs. Hasket Derby ; and no school-girl of our time, writing from Paris or London, could describe the wonders of her tour with greater ecstasy. She sees this new corner of the world with the miracle-working eye of youth, and accepts everything with youth's unquestioning heart. Previous letters had described Salem in terms equally ecstatic, and after her account of the country-seat of the Derbys, there could be nothing left to say of Versailles or St. Cloud. But what then ? Was not this a fine old country-house, with its formal garden, its provincial but still solid stateliness, and, above all, with its hearty, cheerful hospitality ? It was our heroine's first glimpse of the gay world of fashion of her time, and she enjoyed it to the full.

The story of her first meeting with her future husband, of her engagement to him, of their wedding-journey, is told with the simplicity and unaffected candor that were characteristic of her. The letter to her mother in which she asks her consent to the marriage, shows mother and daughter in the happiest light ; it is the highest praise that could be awarded the training the Southgates had given their children. Perfect love had bred perfect confidence, and it is certainly pleasant to know that the hearts and judgments of the parents could only confirm the decision of their daughter. Mr. Walter Bowne was everything that the most exacting parents could wish as the husband of a daughter so dear to them.

---

* Mrs. Rowson's story is well known. She was an Englishwoman, Susanna Haswell, the daughter of an officer in the navy, and was brought to America by her father in 1767, when she was only five years old. Their ship was wrecked on Lovell's Island, in Boston Harbor, and they lived at Nantasket for nearly ten years, when they went back to England. There she married William Rowson, a musician, and went upon the stage. In 1795-96 we find her acting in Baltimore and Boston. She published several comedies and a number of novels ; one of these, " Charlotte Temple," gained great popularity. She died at Boston in 1824. She taught school in several places—at Medford, at Newton, and at Boston, and was very successful.

But the new life of happiness thus entered upon was brief, and in a few months more than six years it had come to an end. In 1803 Mr. Bowne and Miss Southgate were married. In 1806 their first child, a boy, named Walter, after his father, was born ; and two years later, in July, 1808, came their second child, a girl, named Mary, after Mrs. Bowne's mother. After the birth of this child, Mrs. Bowne did not recover her strength, and as winter was coming on, the medical men recommended a sea-voyage and a visit to a warmer climate. It was determined to send the invalid to Charleston, S. C.; and accordingly Mrs. Bowne set out, accompanied by her sister Octavia and her husband, Mr. Browne, leaving Mr. Bowne in New York, where he had some business-affairs to settle before he should join his wife later in the season. Unhappily, the sea-voyage proved a disastrous experiment ; and when the party arrived at Charleston, Mrs. Bowne was in so enfeebled a condition from its effects that her sister gave up all hope of saving her life. She failed rapidly, and died on the 20th of February, only two months after her arrival. Mr. Bowne, who, in common with her family, had probably no idea of the serious nature of his wife's illness when she left New York, yet made all the haste he could to follow her, but had the inexpressible grief to arrive too late. His only consolation was in the fact that her suffering had been brief, and that her departure was serene, while all that a sister's affectionate devotion could avail to comfort her had been given without stint from a full heart ; and even strangers in a strange city had been moved, by the beauty and loveliness of this young mother, and by her pitiful case, deprived of husband and children, to shield her and cheer her with all that the warm-hearted Southern hospitality knows so well to bestow. She was buried in Charleston and her grave was hid in flowers sent by the people of the town and the neighboring plantations, many of whom had only heard her name and story.

THERE is little need for an editor's help in following the story of the life which these letters portray. They are, in fact, an almost complete diary of that life, for the earliest bears date when the writer was a child at boarding-school, and the last was written only a few days before she died. Of the years that came between, the record is almost uninterrupted ; so that the task confided to me resolves itself into little more than a statement of the few facts connected with the personal and family history of their author, that naturally have no place in the letters themselves.

No doubt we have gained much, so far as the material convenience of the great public life is concerned, from the inventions that, for all practical purposes, have reduced time and space to comparative insignificance. We have, however, lost some good things, which those who lived in younger days must always regret, and for which there is small compensation in the material gain we have received in exchange. Among these losses, that of letter-writing is perhaps the most serious. A whole world of innocent enjoyment for contemporaries and for posterity has been blotted out, and, so far as appears, nothing is taking its place. Is it the newspapers? But how scattered, how disjointed, how impersonal, the record they contain ! We might as well hope to recall the charm of some old garden loved in youth, by turning over the leaves of a *herbarium* in which its flowers had been pressed, as to make the domestic life of a time gone by, live again in reading the files of a newspaper. Nor do memoirs or biographies give us what we want. They are too formal, too self-conscious ; they want the spontaneity, the vividness of impression, the lightness of the recording hand. These things letters give us, and letters alone.

Science has many fairy-tales to tell us, but the most magical of all her inventions is that toy, the phonograph, invented by our own Edison. It listens to the words that are whispered in its ear, to the songs that are sung to it, to the gossip that buzzes about it, and the record made on its revolving surface, replaced at any time upon the cylinder—after the lapse of an hour, or of a hundred years—will repeat what has been confided to it in the very voice of the speaker, with every tone and every inflection as clear as when first it spoke.

Familiar letters are privileged to play the same magical part. To the readers of successive generations, they speak with the living voice of the writer ; they recall the fugitive emotions, the joys, the sorrows, the whims, the passions, and as we read we persuade ourselves that we are part and parcel of the times they record.

What a difference in our enjoyment it would make, were the let-

ters of Fanny Burney and Horace Walpole taken from us! Even
Hannah More becomes entertaining ; for though her circle was a
narrow one, there were delightful people in it, and the letters make
us at home in her little world, as no formal biography could do.

Nowadays no one writes letters, and no one would have time
to read them if they were written. Little notes fly back and forth,
like swallows, between friend and friend, between parent and child,
carrying the news of the day in small morsels easily digested ; it
is not worth while to tell the whole story with the pen, when it can
be told in a few weeks, at the farthest, with the voice. For nobody
now is more than a few weeks from anywhere. In the spring my
neighbor came home with his wife from the Philippine Islands, to
pass a few weeks with his friends and hers. Yesterday he ran
back to the islands, to buckle to business again. Why take the
trouble while here to detail the gossip of his home-circle to his
Philippine friends, in letters, when in a fortnight or so he would be
recounting it to them at their own tables ?

The letters here printed have more than the interest of contemporary records ; they paint in words, with a thousand delicate
and expressive touches, the portrait of a lively and beautiful girl,
with a character as striking and individual as the face that Malbone has drawn for us on ivory. Never was a reigning beauty
more spirited, never was a spirited girl of fashion more truly lov-
able, than Eliza Bowne. Whether she be at boarding-school, writing letters to her " honored parents," and hiding her little homesick heart in vain under the formal phrases dictated by the
starched decorum of the day ; or stealing an hour for her pen
amid the whirl of the gay world in which she sparkled, such a
cheerful star, and rattling off to her mother the story of the day's
doings—she is always the same generous, unselfish creature ; im-
pulsive, but with her impulses well in hand ; a heart brimming
over with mirth, its clear crystal clouded by no drop of malice ;
witty, but with a friendly glint in her mischievous eyes, even when,
as now and then happens, she gives formality or presumption a
fillip. Love and friendship followed her wherever she went in her
too brief span of life, and fortune heaped her girlish lap with all
good things ; but she showed herself worthy of her blessings, and
kept herself unspotted from the world.

Something should be said of the literary merit of these letters. The name of Richardson has been mentioned; but Richardson never wrote anything so fresh from the heart, so playful in their sincerity, as some of the letters to her cousin, Moses Porter; nor could Richardson have touched with so light a hand the story of the drive home in the snow-storm after the Assembly ball, or the account of the game of Loo, when, with a fluttering heart, she stands, divided between the eager desire to read the letter she has just slipped into her pocket, and the impatient calls of her partners to join them at the game. Fanny Burney, and Fanny Burney alone, could have written letters like these.

They are not, however, the letters of a practised writer, nor was there ever in her mind any thought of publication. It was the age of "epistolary correspondence:" all the girls of Miss Southgate's acquaintance were writing letters to their friends, long ones, often, made up in the manner of a diary, with a week's doings recorded day by day; for postage was dear, and to send blank paper an extravagance, and no doubt, like her friends, she forgot her letters as soon as they were sent off. Her correspondents were not so indifferent, however, and they kept her letters carefully. Her mother, to whom the most of them were written, left those sent to herself as a bequest to her granddaughter, Mrs. John W. Lawrence, the "little Mary" of the later letters. Mrs. Bowne died in the same year in which this daughter was born; but her sister-in-law, Miss Caroline Bowne, who devoted herself to the care of the little girl after her mother's death, instilled into her heart such an affection for her parent's memory that she came to cherish it with an almost religious devotion, and guarded as a sacred relic everything that had belonged to her. To the letters left her by her grandmother, Mrs. Lawrence added all she could collect from other persons with whom her mother had corresponded. They came to her in a sad state, from much reading and passing about from hand to hand; and to preserve their contents she copied the whole collection, with the greatest care, in her neat, methodical handwriting, into two small books, and these, in her turn, she bequeathed to her children, as her grandmother had bequeathed the originals to her.

They are now given to the public, enriched with a considerable number of contemporary portraits and other illustrations, carefully reproduced from original miniatures and old prints ; and with an abundance of biographical notes, industriously collected by a competent hand, which cannot fail to be of value to the social chronicler of our time. While the importance of these letters as illustrations of the domestic life of our country at a most interesting time is considerable, their chief value, after all, lies in the picture they give of the writer. It is a picture drawn, as we have said, with a thousand graceful touches, and the natural girlish loveliness of the portraiture shows best when it is read from end to end. Then, as we look up from the printed page to Malbone's portrait, the vision takes shape :

> " A hair-brained, sentimental trace
> Was strongly mark'd in her face ;
> A wildly witty, rustic grace
> Shone full upon her ;
> Her eye, even turned on empty space,
> Beamed keen with honour."

CLARENCE COOK.

Fishkill-on-Hudson,
October 1, 1887.

LIST OF ILLUSTRATIONS

MRS. WALTER BOWNE . . . . . Frontispiece
Miniature by Malbone

Facing Page
DR. ROBERT SOUTHGATE—MRS. SOUTHGATE 5
From Silhouettes in the possession of W. B. Lawrence, Esq.

MRS. JOHN DERBY (Eleanor Coffin) . . . 22
Miniature by Malbone, in possession of Miss Rogers, of
Boston

RUFUS KING 42
From a painting by Woods

MRS. RUFUS KING 68
After a portrait by Trumbull

MR. E. HASKET DERBY, OF SALEM (Æt. 28,
1794) 110
From a Miniature in possession of Dr. Hasket Derby, of
Boston

MRS. RICHARD DERBY (Martha Coffin) . . 116
Miniature by Malbone, in possession of Mrs. Peabody, of
Boston

THE VAN RENSSELAER MANOR HOUSE . 130

Facing Page

MR. *WALTER BOWNE* *140*
    Miniature by Malbone

THE *LYMAN PLACE—WALTHAM* . . . *148*

LUCIA WADSWORTH—ZILPAH WADSWORTH *159*
    From Silhouettes in the possession of W. B. Lawrence, Esq.

SUNSWICK—THE DELAFIELD HOUSE, HELL
    GATE, LONG ISLAND *167*

THE *BOWNE HOUSE, FLUSHING* *195*
    Erected 1661

JAMES GORE KING *206*
    From a Miniature in the possession of A. Gracie King, Esq.

CHARLES KING *210*
    From a Miniature in the possession of his daughter, Mrs. Martin.

A GIRL'S LIFE EIGHTY YEARS AGO

Medford, Jan. 23, 1797.

My Mamma:

I went to Boston last Saturday, and there I received your letter. I have now to communicate to you only my wishes to tarry in Boston a quarter, if convenient. In my last letter to my Father I did not say anything respecting it because I did not wish Mrs. Wyman to know I had an inclination to leave her school, but only because I thought you would wish me to come home when my quarter was out. I have a great desire to see my family, but I have a still greater desire to finish my education.

Still I have to beg you to remind my friends and acquaintances that I remain the same Eliza, and that I bear the same love I ever did to them, whether they have forgotten me or not.

Tell my little Brothers and Sisters I want to see them very much indeed. Write me an answer as soon as you can conveniently. I shall send you some of my work which you never have seen, — it is my Arithmetic.

Permit me, my Honored Mother, to claim the title of
Your affectionate daughter,

ELIZA SOUTHGATE.

Mrs. Mary Southgate.

Medford, May 12, 1797.

Honored Parents :

With pleasure I sit down to the best of parents to inform them of my situation, as doubtless they are anxious to hear, — permit me to tell them something of my foolish heart. When I first came here I gave myself up to reflection, but not pleasing reflections. When Mr. Boyd [1] left me I burst into tears and instead of trying to calm my feelings I tried to feel worse. I begin to feel happier and will soon gather up all my Philosophy and think of the duty that now attends me, to think that here I may drink freely of the fountain of knowledge, but I will not dwell any longer on this subject. I am not doing anything but writing, reading, and cyphering. There is a French Master coming next Monday, and he will teach French and Dancing. William Boyd and Mr. Wyman advise me to learn French, yet if I do at all I wish you to write me very soon what you think best, for the school begins on Monday. Mr. Wyman says it will not take up but a very little of my time, for it is but two days in the week, and the lessons only 2 hours long. Mr. Wyman says I must learn Geometry before Geography, and that I better not begin it till I have got through my Cyphering.

We get up early in the morning and make our beds and sweep the chamber, it is a chamber about as large

[1] Joseph Coffin Boyd, of Portland, Maine. Married Isabella, oldest daughter of Dr. Southgate.

DR. ROBERT SOUTHGATE   MRS. SOUTHGATE

From Silhouettes in the possession of W. B. Lawrence, Esq.

as our kitchen chamber, and a little better finished. There's 4 beds in the chamber, and two persons in each bed, we have chocolate for breakfast and supper.

Your affectionate Daughter

ELIZA SOUTHGATE.

Medford, May 25, 1797.

My dear Parents :

I hope I am in some measure sensible of the great obligation I am under to you for the inexpressible kindness and attention which I have received of you from the cradle to my present situation in school. Many have been your anxious cares for the welfare of me, your child, at every stage and period of my inexperienced life to the present moment. In my infancy you nursed and reared me up, my inclinations you have indulged and checked my follies — have liberally fed me with the bounty of your table, and from your instructive lips I have been admonished to virtue, morality, and religion. The debt of gratitude I owe you is great, yet I hope to repay you by duly attending to your counsels and to my improvement in useful knowledge.

> My thankful heart with grateful feelings beat,
> With filial duty I my Parents greet,
> Your fostering care hath reared me from my birth,
> And been my Guardians, since I 've been on earth,
> With love unequalled taught the surest way,
> And Check'd my passions when they went astray.
> I wish and trust to glad declining years, —
> Make each heart gay — each eye refrain from tears.

When days are finished and when time shall cease
May you be wafted to eternal peace

Is the sincere wish of your dutiful Daughter,

ELIZA SOUTHGATE.

Robert Southgate Esqr. & Lady.

Medford, June 13, 1797.

Dear Mother:

With what pleasure did I receive your letter and hear the praises of an approving Mother! It shall be my study to please and make you happy. You said you hoped that I was not disappointed in learning French; I hope you think that I have too much *love* and *reverence* for my Parents to take any thing amiss that *they* thought most proper for me. I was very happy to hear that you had received the bonnets, and I hope they will suit you. I have never received a letter from Horatio[1] since I have been here. I expect to begin Geometry as soon as I have done Cyphering, which I

[1] Horatio Southgate, Dr. Southgate's oldest son, followed the profession of the law in the town of Portland, Maine, and was for twenty-one years Register of Probate for Cumberland County, Maine. Mr. Southgate married three times. His first wife was a friend of his sisters and was Abigail McLellan, the daughter of Hugh McLellan, a well-known East Indian merchant. Mary Webster was Mr. Southgate's second wife; she was the daughter of Noah Webster, whose name is well known in connection with the dictionary that he wrote. Mr. Southgate's third wife was Eliza Neal of Portland. By his three wives Mr. Southgate had a large family of children, among them being the Rt. Rev'd Horatio Southgate and the Rev'd William Scott Southgate.

hope will be soon, for I have got as far as Practice. Tell Isabella[1] and Mama[2] King, that some letters from them would give me great pleasure and that I hope to experience it soon. I should have written to Mama King, but I had not time, but I intend to, the first opportunity. I have found the nubs and sent them to Portland. I received your letter by my Brother Boyd, and was very much surprised to hear that Octavia[3] was going to have the small-pox. Please to give my love to Harriet Emerson, and Mary Rice, and tell them that I intend to write to them very soon and shall expect some letters from them. Give my love to all my friends and tell them that I often think on them, and I hope they will not forget your affectionate daughter

ELIZA SOUTHGATE.

Mrs. Mary Southgate.

Medford, August 11, 1797.

Dear Parents :

It is a long time since I received a letter from home, and I have neglected my duty in not writing to you oftener. I shall send you with this some of my Pieces,

---

[1] Isabella Southgate had married to Joseph Coffin Boyd. She was Dr. Southgate's oldest child.

[2] Mary Black, the second wife of Richard King, Mrs. Southgate's stepmother. She had married Mr. King soon after the death of his first wife, who was her cousin, and had been a kind and devoted mother to his three children.

[3] Octavia Southgate, Dr. Southgate's third daughter. She married, in 1805, William Browne.

and you will see if you think I have improved any : the
Epitaph on the Hon. Thomas Russell was the first one
that I wrote. My brother Boyd never came to see me
when he was up, only called and delivered me the letter.
I have never heard any thing since from Boston, nor
seen any of my acquaintance from there. I have not
been to Boston since Election. I expected to have gone
to Commencement, but I did not. I fear that the time
allotted for my stay here will be too short for me to go
so far as I wish, for I shall have to go much farther in
Arithmetic than I had an idea of, then go over it again
in a large book of my own writing ; for my Instructor
does not wish to give me a superficial knowledge only.
He says if I am very diligent ; he thinks that 9 months
from the time I came will *do*, if I can't stay longer ; I
should feel happy, and very grateful, if you thought
proper to let me tarry that time. I have Cyphered now
farther than Isabella did, for I have been thro' Practice,
the Rule of Three and Interest and two or three rules
that I never did before.

I would thank you to write me word if you are willing
for me to stay so long. With wishing you health and
all the happiness which you are capable of enjoying,
permit me to subscribe myself

Your affectionate and most dutiful Daughter

ELIZA SOUTHGATE.

Mr. & Mrs. Southgate.

Medford, Aug. 14, 1797.

Dear Mother:

I am very sorry for your trouble, and sympathize with you in it. I now regret being from home, more than ever, for I think I might be of service to you now the children are sick. I hope they will be as much favored in their sickness *now*, as they were when they had the measles. I am very sorry that Jane has broken her arm, for it generally causes a long confinement, and I fear she has not got patience enough to bear it without a great deal of trouble. I suppose that Isabella will be very much worried about her babe. I would thank you to write me very often now — for I shall be very anxious about the children. I believe I have got some news to tell you, that is, I have found one of your acquaintance, and relation; it is a Mrs. *Sawyer*, before she was married she was Polly King, and she says that you kept at their house when you was in Boston. I believe I have nothing more to request, only for you to give my love to all the children, and *kiss* each of them for *me*, and tell them to be as patient as they can. Give my respects to my Father and tell him I want to receive a letter from him very much.

I am your affectionate and dutiful daughter

ELIZA SOUTHGATE.

Mrs. Mary Southgate.

Medford, August 25, 1797.

Dear Mother :

I received your packet of things the 20th inst. and was very glad of them. If you will be so kind as to send me word whether Sarah's[1] ear-rings were in the basket, I will be much obliged to you. I have forgotten whether I did or not — write me word if you like your bonnet and the children's, I hope you do.

Give my love to Sarah and all the children, and kiss Arixene,[2] and Robert for me. Never did I know the worth of good parents half so much as now I am from them ; I never missed our closet so much, and above all things our cheese and Butter which we have but very little of, but I am very contented. I wish you would send me up my patterns all of them for I want them very much indeed, for I expect to work me a gown.

I am with due respect

Your dutiful daughter

ELIZA SOUTHGATE.

Mrs. Mary Southgate.

[1] Sarah Leland was the daughter of Mrs. Southgate's half-sister Dorcas King, Mrs. Joseph Leland.

[2] Arixene and Robert Southgate, Eliza's younger sister and brother. Arixene married Henry Smith, of Sacarappa, Maine.

Medford, Sept. 30, 1797.

Dear Mother:

You mentioned in yours, of the 16th inst. that it was a long time since you had received a letter from me; but it was owing to my studies which took up the greater part of my time; for I have been busy in my Arithmetic, but I finished it yesterday, and expect now to begin my large manuscript Arithmetic. You say that you shall regret so long an absence; not more certainly than I shall, but a strong desire to possess more useful knowledge than I at present do, I can dispense with the pleasure a little longer of beholding my friends and I hope I shall be better prepared to meet my good parents towards whom my heart overflows with gratitude. You mentioned in your letter about my Winter clothes of which I will make out a Memorandum. I shall want a coat and you may send it up for me to make, or you may make it your self, but I want it made loose with a belt. I wish you to send me enough of all my slips to make long sleeves that you can, and I wish you would pattern my dark slip to make long sleeves. I want a flannel waist, and a petticoat, for my white one dirts so quick that I had rather have a colored one. I have nothing more to write, only give my love to all who ask after me. I have just received a letter from Horatio, he is very well.

Your ever affectionate daughter
ELIZA SOUTHGATE.

Mrs. Mary Southgate.

Medford, Oct. 17, 1797.

Dear Brother:

Yours of the 11th of Sept. was gratefully received by your affectionate Sister; and your excuse at first I thought not very good, but now I think it very good, for I have been plagued very much myself. William Boyd came from Portland about a fortnight since and by him I was informed that Sister Isabella's child was very sick and he was in doubt whether it would ever get over it. I feel for Isabella much more than I can tell you who is but just entered the bonds of Matrimony should so soon have sickness, and perhaps Death, be one of the guests of her family. I was also informed that the children had all got over the hooping cough and that Octavia was much healthier than she was before she had the small-pox. By my last letter from home Papa informed me that I might tarry all Winter and I have concluded to. I suppose you would like to know how I spend my time here. I shall answer, very well; my going abroad is chiefly in Boston, for I don't go out much in Medford. It was vacation about a week since and I spent it in Boston very agreeably.

I keep at Mr. Boyd's when I am there, and Mrs. Little's. I go to Boston every public day as Mr. B. is so good as to send for me. I am very fond of that family and likewise Mrs. Little's. You speak of my writing and you think that I have improved. I am glad of it.

I hope I shall make as great progress in my other studies and be an " Accomplished Miss."

Horatio do write very soon ; will you ?

Adieu ! your affectionate Sister

ELIZA SOUTHGATE.

Horatio Southgate.

Medford, Nov. 10, 1797.

You mentioned in your letter, my dear mother, that Cousin Mary informed you that I expected to go to the Ball.   I did think that I should go but I altered my mind ; I had 2 or 3 invitations but I would not accept of any of them.   My cloak likewise you mentioned something about, which I shall attend to when I go to Boston.   I expect to go to Boston at Thanksgiving, for there is a vacation of a week.   I had a letter from *Horatio* yesterday, he was well.   Isabella wrote me word that my Father had got the Rheumatism very bad, which I am sorry to hear.   If the wishes or prayers of Eliza would heal the wound, it would not long remain unheal'd.

My love to all the children, tell them I don't dare to tell them how much I want to see them, nor even think. My love to all that ask after me.   May all the happiness that is possible for you to enjoy be experienced is the sincere wish of

Your affectionate Daughter

ELIZA S.

Mrs. Mary Southgate.

Medford, Dec. 16, 1797.

My Dear Father:

I received yours with pleasure and was happy to hear that you were better. I hope you will continue growing better until the complaint is entirely removed. I came from Boston yesterday after spending vacation there. I went to the theater the night before for the first time, and Mr. Turner came into the box where I was. I did not know him at first, neither did he me, but he soon found me out. With this I shall send some pieces. My respect is justly due to my good Mother, and my love to all who ask after me, the children in particular. I hope to improve to your satisfaction, which will amply reward me for all my pains.

I must conclude with wishing you health and happiness.

Your ever affectionate daughter,   E. S.

Medford, Jan'y 9th, 1798.

My Good Father:

The contents of your letter surprised me at first; it may sometimes be of service to me, for while I have such a monitor, I never can act contrary to such advice. No, my Father, I hope by the help of Heaven never to cause shame or misery to attend the grey hairs of my Parents nor myself, but on the contrary to *glad* your declining years with happiness and that you may never have cause to rue the day that gave me existence. My heart feels no attachment except to my family. I respect many of my friends but *love* none but my Parents. Your letter shall be my guide from home, and when I again behold our own peaceful mansion then will I again be guided by my Parents' happiness, — their happiness shall be my pursuit. My heart overflows with gratitude toward you and my good Mother. I am sensible of the innumerable obligations I am under to you. You mention in your letter about my pieces, which you say you imagine are purloined; I am very sorry if they are, for I set more by them than any of my pieces ; one was the Mariner's Compass, and the other was a Geometrical piece. I spent Thanksgiving at Mrs. Little's and Christmas here. I have finished my large Manuscript Arithmetic and want to get it bound, and then I shall send it to you. I have done a small Geometry book and shall begin a large one to-morrow, such a one as you saw at Mr. Wyman's if you remember. It is the beginning of a new year ; allow me then to pay you the compliments of the season. — I pray that this year to you may prove a year of health, prosperity, and love. My quarter will be out the 8th day of next month, it will be in about four weeks. I wish you would write me soon how I am to come home — for I wish to know.

I should be very glad if *you* could make it convenient to come for me, for I wish *you* to come. Give my love to Irene and tell her I believe she owes me a letter; if you please you may tell her that part of my letter which concerns school affairs.

My love is due to all who will take the trouble to ask after me. Tell Mamma I have begun the turban and will send it as soon as I finish it. When I see her I will tell her why I did not do it before.

Accept my sincere wishes that My Parents may enjoy all the happiness that ever mortals know.

Still I hope I am

Your *dutiful* Daughter,

ELIZA SOUTHGATE.

Robert Southgate, Esq.

Boston, Jan. 30, 1798.

My Honored Father:

By Capt. Bradbury I was informed that you wished me to come home with him, which I should have complied with, had not I have seen my Uncle William [1] to-day, and he informed me that you had concluded to let me spend some time in Boston, which I was very glad to hear. I shall now wait until I hear certain, which I wish you to send me word by the next post. — I shall enclose in this a card of Mrs. Rawson's terms which

---

[1] William King, the son of Richard King by his second wife Mary Black, was a large land-owner near the town of Bath. Mr. King was elected the first Governor when the District of Maine was changed into a State with a government of its own.

you may peruse ; until then I remain with the same affection,

Your dutiful Daughter, Eliza S.

Boston, February 13, 1798.

Hon. Father :

I am again placed at school under the tuition of an amiable lady, so mild, so good, no one can help loving her ; she treats all her scholars with such a tenderness as would win the affection of the most savage brute, tho' scarcely able to receive an impression of the kind. I learn Embroidery and Geography at present and wish your permission to learn Musick. You may justly say, my best of Fathers, that every letter of mine is one which is asking for something more ; never contented — I only ask, if you refuse me, I know you do what you think best, and I am sure I ought not to complain, for you have never yet refused me anything that I have asked, my best of Parents, how shall I repay you? You answer, by your good behaviour. Heaven grant that it may be such as may repay you. A year will have rolled over my head before I shall see my Parents. I have ventured from them at an early age to be so long a time absent, but I hope I have learnt a good lesson by it — a lesson of experience, which is the best lesson I could learn.

I have described one of the blessings of creation in Mrs. Rawson, and now I will describe Mrs. Wyman as the reverse : she is the worst woman I ever knew of all that I ever saw ; nobody knows what I suffered from the treatment of that woman — I had the misfortune to be a favorite with Miss Haskell and Mr. Wyman, she said, and she treated me as her own malicious heart dictated ; but whatever is, is right, and I learnt a good lesson by it. I wish you, my Father, to write an answer soon and let me know if I may learn music. — Give my best respects to my good Mother, tho' what I say to my Father applies to my Mother as much as to my Father. May it please the disposer of all events to return me safe home to the bosom of my friends in health safely. I never was happier in my life I think, and my heart overflows toward my heavenly Father for it ; and may it please him to continue it and afford it to my Parents, is the sincere wish of

Your   Eliza Southgate.

Robert Southgate, Esqr.

Boston, May 12th, 1798.

My dear Parents :

Now at the end of the week, when my hopes are almost exhausted of seeing my brother, I attempt to address you, — a task which was once delightful but now painful since my Mother's last letter. I see my errors, and if I can hope they will no longer be remembered by my Parents, I shall again be happy.

My Mother's letter greatly surprised me after having

received so different a one from my Father. Indeed, my Parents, did you think I would any longer cherish a passion *you* disapproved? After expressing your disapprobation it was enough, your *wishes are* and ever shall be my commands. I have spent a week of painful expectation; no letter, no brother, no father have come, and I am now in anxious expectation to receive a letter to-night, but I dare not hope it to be so. Do, my Father, as soon as you receive this send for me as soon as possible, for my quarter at Mrs. Rawson's was out last Saturday, and as circumstances are, I thought it proper not to go to Mr. Boyd's. I beg of you to send for me home directly, for I only board at Mrs. Rawson's now, for I am in expectation of seeing or hearing every day and therefore I have not begun any more work. My time is spending without gain. I am at Mrs. Frazier's and have been here ever since Thursday. I shall go back to Mrs. Rawson's to-night and there wait for further orders. Time hangs more heavy than ever it did before. I am with the most sincere Respect and affection

Your daughter   ELIZA.

R. & M. Southgate.

Scarborough, Dec. 16th.

I am sorry to have given Aunt Porter such an opportunity of charging me with neglect in executing her commission, but I can easily convince her I did not deserve censure; for until last Friday I never received yours of Nov. 22nd, and I shall execute that part of Aunt's request which I can in Scarborough — the gown patterns I shall enclose. The one with a fan back is meant to just meet before and pin the Robings, no string belt or any thing. The other pattern is a plain waist with strips of the same sticked on, and for white, laced between with bobbin or cord. I have a muslin done so with black silk cord, which looks very handsome — and I have altered my brown silk into one like the other pattern. I was over at Saco yesterday and saw one Mary [King] had made in Boston. It was a separate waist, or rather the breadths did not go quite up. The waist was plain with one stripe of cording let in behind and the rest of the waist perfectly plain — the skirt part was plaited in box plaits 3 of a side — which reached to the shoulder strap and only enough left to meet strait before, as is one of the patterns I have sent. You ask so many questions that I hardly know how to answer them. Isabella is almost recovered — her family well. The baby I believe will be named Charles Orlando. The assemblies begin next Thursday — as also do Saco assemblies, and on Friday I go to the Saco assembly — probably I shall go to next Portland assembly. You ask how Mr. Little and Laura do? A strange question. Laura is well or was last Thursday, and Mr. Little is soon to be married to Miss Bowman of Exeter.

Papa has been confined to the house a week yesterday by a wound on his leg which he made with an axe, he wounded the tendon which leads from his great toe up, he cut it a little above the ankle — it has been very painful. Give my love to Aunt, tell her I shall not be able to come down this winter, for my next visit will be to Boston. Write me the next opportunity respecting the sables, and the time and how Uncle goes to Boston that I may be in readiness.

Family all well. Eliza.

To Octavia.

Boston, Feb. 7th, 1800.

After the toil, the bustle and fatigue of the week I turn towards home to relate the manner in which I have spent my time. I have been continually engaged in parties, plays, balls, &c. &c. Since the first week I came to town, I have attended all the balls and assemblies, one one week and one the next. They have regular balls once a fortnight, so that I have been to one or the other every Thursday. They are very brilliant, and I have formed a number of pleasing acquaintances there; last night, which was ball night, I drew No. 5, & 2nd sett drew a Mr. Snow, bad partner; danced voluntarily with Mr. Oliver, Mr. Andrews, Mr. McPherson; danced until 1 o'clock; they have charming suppers, table laid entirely with china. I had charming partners always. To-day I intended going to Mrs. Codman's, engaged to a week ago, but wrote a billett I was indisposed, but the truth of the matter was that I wanted to go to the play to see Bunker hill, and Uncle (William King) wished I should — therefore I shall go. I have engagements for the greater part of next week. To-morrow we all go to hear Fisher Ames' Eulogy. And in the morning going to look at some instruments; however we got one picked out that I imagine we shall take, 150 dollars — a charming toned one and not made in this country. I am still at Mrs. Frazier's, she treats me with the greatest attention. Nancy is indeed a charming girl, — I have the promise of her company the ensuing summer. I have bought me a very handsome skirt, white satin. Richard Cutts went shopping with me yesterday morn, engaged to go to the play next week with him. For mourning for Washington the ladies dress as much as if for a relation, some entirely in black, but now many wear only a ribbon with a line painted on it. I have not yet been out to see Mrs. Rawson and Miss Haskell, but intend to next week. Uncle William [King] has been very attentive to me — carried me to the play 3 or 4 times and to all the balls and assemblies excepting the last which I went with Mr. Andrews. Give my best respects to Pappa and Mamma, and tell them I shall soon be tired of this dissipated life and almost want to go home already. I have a line to write to Mary Porter and must conclude.

To Octavia.   ELIZA.

MRS. JOHN DERBY. (ELEANOR COFFIN.)

Miniature by Malbone, in possession of Miss Rogers of Boston.

ARTOTYPE, E BIERSTADT, N. Y.

Now Mamma, what do you think I am going to ask for ? — a wig.   Eleanor [1] has got a new one just like my hair and only 5 dollars, Mrs. Mayo one just like it.   I must either cut my hair or have one, I cannot dress it at all *stylish*.   Mrs. Coffin bought Eleanor's and says that she will write to Mrs. Sumner to get me one just like it ; how much time it will save — in one year we could save it in pins and paper, besides the *trouble*.   At the assembly I was quite ashamed of my head, for nobody has long hair.   If you will consent to my having one do send me over a 5 dollar bill by the post immediately after you receive this, for I am in hopes to have it for the next Assembly — do send me word immediately if you can let me have one.   Tell Octavia she must write soon, and that there are many inquiries after her.

ELIZA.

To Octavia Southgate — Mrs. Frazier's.

12th of June, 1800.
Hanover Street, Boston.

In the Hospital !   Bless your heart, I am not there ! Who told you I was ?   Mr. Davis I know, if you see him tell him I shall scold him for it.   Martha has heard the

---

[1] Eleanor Coffin, afterwards Mrs. John Derby, was the daughter of Dr. Coffin, a neighbor of Dr. Southgate's.   Martha Coffin, another daughter, had lately married Mr. Richard Derby.   The Mrs. Codman mentioned in the previous letter was a sister of Dr. Coffin's.

same; true I had some idea of going in, but gave it up as soon as I heard Dr. Coffin did not attend. Horatio did likewise. Your last to Mamma is dated from Mrs. Frazier's; how, Octavia, shall we discharge the debt of gratitude which we owe her? it had exceeded my hopes of payment before you went, surely it is now doubled. You mention nothing of any letters from me; I have written several and in one told you particularly that Mamma wished you by all means to take lessons in music; you don't tell us what you have done since you have been in Medford. Martha writes me that you are to spend part of vacation at Mrs. Sumner's. What has become of Ann and Harriett? I am out of patience waiting for them, why don't they write, it is an age since I have had one line. Col. Boyd I hope will bring some letters from all of you. I have heard that Eleanor Coffin received attentions from Sam Davis when in Boston, did you hear of it? Martha writes me too that Mr. Andrews is paying attention to a young lady in Boston, but does not mention her name, *Miss Packman* I guess; he was said to be her swain last winter. Mary Porter went home last week, I went with her, she has now gone to Topsham to tarry until uncle returns. I anxiously expect a letter from Ann or Harriett to know the reason that they don't hasten their visit. I am learning my 12th tune, Octavia, I almost worship my Instrument, — it reciprocates my sorrows and joys, and is my bosom companion. How I long to have you return! I have hardly attempted to sing since you went away. I am sure I shall not dare to when you return. I must enjoy my triumph while you are absent; my musical talents will be dim when compared with the lustre of yours. Pooh, Eliza, you are not envious? no! I will excel in something else if not in music. Oh nonsense, this spirit of emulation in families is destructive of concord and harmony, at least I will endeavor to excel you in *sisterly affection.* If you outshine me in accomplishments, will it not be all in the family? Certainly. How I wish I had a *balloon,* I would see you and all my friends in Boston in a trice. I have not got one. Do tell me is Ann the same dear good friend and as much my *sister romp* as ever? Tell her I am so affronted with her that I won't speak to her. Sister Boyd is over, won't go home this week; about your work, I will go down stairs and ask Mamma, — a *mourning piece* with a figure in it, and two other pictures, *mates* — figures of females I think handsomer than Landscapes. Mrs. Rawson knows what is best, — thus says Mamma — she don't wish any screens. Mr. Little, the bearer of this, another beau I send you, and here is poor *I* not a bit of a one, *Doc. Bacon* excepted, and even *him, Cousin Mary,* selfish creature, has lugged off his *heart* and left the remainder here, so we might as well have a stump — poor soul, his face looks like a *Piana,*[1] one continued blush — I suppose for fear of hearing her name mentioned, and she, unreasonable creature! thinks he is not all perfection. Unaccountable taste! he is very *delightsome* surely, — how

1 Peony (vulgarly called Piny). Note by M. B. L.

long shall I rant at this rate. I long to go to Portland
and then I shall see some being that looks like a beau —
or a monkey, or anything you please ; — To supply the
loss I often look out the window, till my imagination
forms one out of a tree or anything that I see, we can
imagine anything you know. Bless my soul, Mr. L. is
waiting!   ELIZA.

Give my love, respects, everything, to all.

July 3rd, 1800.

I believe, my Dear Mother, that you meant to give me
a very close lesson in Economy — when you cut out the
shirts for me to make. You had measured off the
bodies of two and cut them part way in — and also the
sleeves were marked, — after I had cut them off there
was a quarter of a yard left. I now wanted the collars
and all the trimmings. I made out after a great deal of
planning to get out the shoulder pieces, — wrist-bands,
I pair of neck gussets and one of sleeve do., are still
wanting. I shall send this on by Mrs. Smith, and if you
can find out when she returns I wish you would send
some linen and some more shirts to make as I shall soon
finish these, and can as well finish making up the piece
here as at home. I was very sorry I did not wear my
habit down as I shall want it when I go to Wiscassett.
If you can possibly find an opportunity, I wish you
would send it to me. Aunt Porter's child is one of the
most troublesome ones I ever saw, he cries continually,

and she is at present destitute of any help except a little girl about 12 years old. I wish, my Dear Mother, that you would forward all letters that come to Scarborough for me immediately. I hope you will enjoy yourself in Portland this week. I was almost tempted to wish to stay a week there, — there were so many parties, and so gay every body appeared — that I longed to stay and take part. I forgot all about it before I got to Topsham, — much as I enjoy society I never am unhappy when without it, — I cannot but feel happy that I was brought up in retirement, — since from habit at least, I have contracted a love for solitude, I never feel alone when I have my pen or my book. I feel that I ought to be very happy in the company of such a woman as Aunt Porter, for I really don't know any one whose mind is more improved, and which makes her both a useful and instructing companion. Her sentiments and opinions are more like those I have formed than any person I know of. I think my disposition like hers, and I feel myself drawn towards her by an irresistible impulse, not an hour but she reminds me of you and I sincerely think her more like you than your own sister. I shall write you when I go farther East. I don't know what I shall do about writing Octavia, as Mrs. Rawson told her I wrote on an improper subject when I asked her in my letter if Mr. Davis was paying attention to Eleanor Coffin, and she would not let her answer the question. This is *refining* too much, and if I can't write as I feel, I can't write at all. Now I ask you, Mamma, if it is not quite a natural question when we hear that any of our friends are paid attention to by any gentleman, to ask a confirmation of the report from those we think most likely to know the particulars. Never did I write a line to Octavia but I should have been perfectly willing for you or my Father to have seen. You have always treated me more like a companion than a daughter, and therefore would make allowance for the volatile expressions I often make use of. I never felt the least restraint in company with my Parents which would induce me to stifle my gaiety, and you have kindly permitted me to rant over all my nonsense uncorrected, and I positively believe it has never injured. I must bid you good-night.   ELIZA.

Pray don't forget to send some more shirts.

July 17, 1800.

I must again trouble my Dear Mother by requesting her to send on my spotted muslin. A week from next Saturday I set out for Wiscassett, in company with Uncle William and Aunt Porter. Uncle will fetch Ann [1] to meet us there, and as she has some acquaintance there we shall stay some time and aunt will leave us and return to Topsham ; so long a visit in Wiscassett will oblige me to muster all my muslins, for I am informed they are so monstrous smart as to take no notice of any

[1] Ann, daughter of Cyrus King (Mrs. Southgate's half-brother) and his wife Hannah Stone. She was named after her aunt, Mrs. William King, Ann Frazier. She afterwards married Mr. Bridge.

lady that can condescend to wear a calico gown, therefore, dear mother, to ensure me a favorable reception, pray send my spotted muslin by the next mail after you receive this, or I shall be on my way to Wiscassett. I shall go on horseback, — how I want my habit, — I wish it had not been so warm when I left home and I should have worn it. I am in hopes you will find an opportunity to send it by a private conveyance before I go, but my muslin you must certainly send by the mail. Aunt Porter's little Rufus is very sick, poor child, he was born under an evil star. I believe Pandora opened her box upon him when he first came into existence. The mumps, I believe, now afflict him; night before last we were alarmed about him for fear of his having the Quinsy, but I believe he is in no danger of that now. I wish to hear from home very much. ELIZA.

I shall anxiously await the arrival of the next mail after you receive this.

Scarborough, Sept. 14, 1800.

I suppose I ought to commence my letter with an humble apology, begging forgiveness for past offences and promising to do better in future, but no, I will only tell you that I have been so much engaged since I got home from Topsham that I could not write you. Martha tells us you were in Boston last Sunday. Mamma thinks, Octavia, you are there too much, we do not know how often, but we hear of you there very often indeed. I

think, my dear sister, you ought to improve every moment of your time, which is short, very short to complete your education.   In November terminates the period of your instruction.   The last you will receive perhaps ever, only what you may gain by observation.
You will never cease to learn I hope, the world is a volume of instruction, which will afford you continual employment, — peruse it with attention and candor and you
will never think the time thus employed misspent.   I
think, Octavia, I would not leave my school again until
you finally leave it.   You may — you will think this is
harsh; you will not always think so ; remember those
that wish it must know better what is proper than you
possibly can.   Horatio will come on for you as soon as
your quarter is out.   We anticipate the time with pleasure; employ your time in such a manner as to make
your improvements conspicuous.   A boarding-school, I
know, my dear Sister, is not like home, but reflect a moment, is it not necessary, *absolutely necessary* to be more
strict in the government of 20 or 30 young ladies, nearly
of an age and different dispositions, than a private family ?   Your good sense will easily tell you it is.   No
task can be greater than the care of so many girls, it is
impossible not to be *partial*, but we may conceal our
partiality.   I should have a poor opinion of any person
that did not feel a love for merit, superior to what they
can for the world in general.   I should never approve
of such general love.   I say this not because I think
you are discontented, far from it — your letters tell us

quite the reverse and I believe it. Surely, Octavia, you must allow that no woman was ever better calculated to govern a school than Mrs. Rawson. She governs by the love with which she always inspires her scholars. You have been indulged, Octavia, so we have all. I was discontented when I first went from home. I dare say you have had some disagreeable sensations, yet your reason will convince you, you ought not to have had. You had no idea when you left home of any difference in your manner of living. I knew you would easily be reconciled to it and therefore said but little to you about it. Yesterday Miss Haskell's letter, which I so much wished for and so highly prize, was sent me; tell her to trust no more letters to the politeness of Mr. Jewett,[1] for he will forget to deliver them; he has been studying in the same office with Horatio ever since he returned and never told him he had a letter for me till I told Horatio to ask him. I did get it at last and will answer it as soon as I have an opportunity, which I expect soon, my letters are of too little consequence to send by Post. Tell Miss Haskell how highly I am obliged to her for every letter, and how much it gratifies me to have her write thus. My love and esteem ever awaits our good Mrs. Rawson, and hope she does not intend my last letter shall go unanswered. Susan Wyman is still remem-

---

[1] Mr. Jewett married Sally Weeks, a friend and neighbor of the Misses Southgate. He was a grandson of Aaron Jewett, who built the first saw-mill on Algers Falls, Dunstan, in 1727, and carried on what was then considered an extensive lumber business.

bered as the companion of my amusements in Medford.
Irene joins me in love to her.   Betsey Bloom my love to
her likewise. — Family are all well, Octavia, Sister Boyd
is here, been with us several days.   Let us hear from you
when you have an opportunity.   I should like to know
how many tunes you play, but you have never answered
any of my enquiries of this kind, therefore I suppose I
ought not to make them.   Your   ELIZA.
    Octavia.

                                    Scarborough, Sept. 14, 1800.

    Tired, stupid, and sleepy, I feel that I can write noth-
ing instructive or amusing.   Oh these *summer balls* are
not the thing, but it was much more comfortable than
I expected.   My ears were continually assailed with
lamentations that you were not present.   Mr. Kinsman
would certainly have gone out for you (so he said) had
he ever been at our house.   He really asked one or two
gentlemen to go.   He is a frothy fellow.   He rattles
without a spark of fancy and stuns you with his volu-
bility, as anything hollow or empty always makes the
most noise.   I told him I received a letter from you
yesterday.   He gave a pious ejaculation to heaven,
turned gracefully on his heel and entreated in the most
humble manner that I would grant him a sight of one
line !   I refused as I thought him too insignificant an
animal to be so much honored.   Col. Boyd arrived last
night, I found him in the parlor when I went down to

breakfast, he enquired for you. Mr. Derby and Mr. Coffin will leave town to-day or to-morrow for Boston, they undoubtedly will call and see you. 'Twill be a good opportunity to send me the money if Mamma pleases. Harriet will sail to-morrow or next day, she sends an abundance of love.   ELIZA.
   Octavia.

Bath, October, Sunday.

After a fortnight very pleasantly spent in Wiscassett I return to Bath. In my last I mentioned that Judge Lowell's family were expected in Wiscassett; they came immediately after, and Eliza, the youngest, brought letters from Ellen Coffin, thus I very readily got acquainted with them. Judge Lowell appears to be one of the mildest, most amiable men I ever saw. Mrs. Lowell is a fine ladylike woman, yet her manners are such as would have been admired 50 years ago, there is too much appearance of whalebone and buckram to please the depraved taste of the present age. Nanny L., the oldest daughter, is animated, sensible, enthusiastic, and very easy and pleasing in her conversation and manners, you would be delighted with her conversation — 'tis elegant and refined, she has no airs. Eliza is a little, charming, sweet creature, she is about 17 or 18, short, fat, and a blooming complexion, handsome blue eyes, light hair, beautiful dimples, artless and unaffected in her manners, — indeed I was delighted with her, she is so perfectly amiable in her

appearance.   I was much pleased at an acquaintance
with them.   At Wiscassett I was invited to accompany
them to Bath, as they were going in a boat.   I accepted
with pleasure.   In the morning, which was Monday,
they called for me and I went with them as far as
Tincham's where they kept; at last, after a long debate,
it was thought too hazardous to go by water while the
wind blew so violently, 'twas determined to go by land.
Mr. Lee took the two Miss Lowells and myself in his
carriage, which holds 4 very charmingly.   Judge Lowell
and wife in a chaise with a boy to carry it back.   Judge
Bourne in a chair with a boy, and Mr. Merrill on horseback.   About 5 miles on our way Mr. Lee took Mr.
Merrill's horse and he sat in with us, and he sang us a
number of songs; we had a charming time.   At the ferry
Mr. Lee, Mr. Merrill, and the boys with the chaise left
us; we then all got into a boat and landed at Uncle's
wharf; 'tis about 3 miles, a most charming sail, indeed
we had a very pleasant time.   They went directly to
Page's, and in the evening I went up to see them; left
them at 8 and with real regret.   I had passed several
pleasant hours in their society.   They set out in the
morning for Portland.   Only think of Eleanor going to
be married; 'tis no more than I expected and believed
at the moment I heard it.   Poor Mrs. Sumner, what an
afflicting loss she has met with, my heart bleeds while I
think how *very fond* she was of the little creature, she
was a lovely child.   How do all do at home?   I long to
get home, I never wanted to see home more in my life,

yet I am very happy here. I wish Mamma would send me two of my cotton shifts and my habit or great-coat to ride home in; send them by Uncle. Pray get the instrument tuned. If you see Moses[1] soon tell him I think it impossible to find words to express my obligation to him for his many and long letters, yet I shall endeavour to convince him I have a due sense of them. I shall make all the return in my power. I was going up to Topsham this week. I wish to very much, but Mamma King and Uncle both going, Nanny would be quite alone, I must stay to comfort her. As to Aunt Porter I believe she will think I am never coming to Topsham. I begin to think so myself, but what am I to do? However I must. I shall go as soon as Uncle returns and stay till I return home. I want to see Aunt Porter very much. Write me soon and tell me what news you hear. Love to all. Is Pappa gone to Salem?

ELIZA.

To Octavia Southgate.

To Moses Porter.

My most charming Cousin! Most kind and condescending friend — teach me how I may express the grateful sense I have of the obligations I owe you; your many and long letters have chased away the spleen, they have rendered me cheerful and happy, and I almost

[1] Moses Porter was Eliza's cousin. He was the oldest son of Mrs. Aaron Porter (Paulina King).

forgot I was so far from home. — O shame on you! Moses, you know I hate this formality among friends, you know how gladly I would throw all these fashionable forms from our correspondence; but you still oppose me, you adhere to them with as much scrupulosity as to the ten commandments, and for aught I know you believe them equally essential to the salvation of your soul. But, Eliza, you have not answered my last letter! True, and if I had not have answered it, would you never have written me again — and I confess that I believe you would not — yet I am mortified and displeased that you value my letters so little, that the exertions to continue the correspondence must all come from me, that if I relax my zeal in the smallest degree it may drop to the ground without your helping hand to raise it. I do think you are a charming fellow, — would not write because I am in debt, well, be it so, my ceremonious friend, — I submit, and though I transgress by sending a half sheet more than you ever did, yet I assure you 'twas to convince you of the violence of my anger which could *induce* me to forget the rules of politeness. I am at Wiscassett. I have seen Rebecca every day, she is handsome as ever, and we both of us were in constant expectation of seeing you for 2 or 3 days, you did not come and we were disappointed.

I leave here for Bath next week. I have had a ranting time, and if I did not feel so offended, I would tell you more about it.

As I look around me I am surprised at the happiness
which is so generally enjoyed in families, and that mar-
riages which have not love for a foundation on more
than one side at most, should produce so much apparent
harmony. I may be censured for declaring it as my
opinion that not one woman in a hundred marries for
love. A woman of taste and sentiment will surely see
but a very few whom she could love, and it is altogether
uncertain whether either of them will particularly distinguish her. If they should, surely she is very fortunate, but it would be one of fortune's random favors
and such as we have no right to expect. The female
mind I believe is of a very pliable texture; if it were
not we should be wretched indeed. Admitting as a
known truth that few women marry those whom they
would prefer to all the world if they could be viewed by
them with equal affection, or rather that there are often
others whom they could have preferred if they had felt
that affection for them which would have induced them
to offer themselves, — admitting this as a truth not to
be disputed, — is it not a subject of astonishment that
happiness is not almost banished from this connexion?
Gratitude is undoubtedly the foundation of the esteem
we commonly feel for a husband. One that has preferred us to all the world, one that has thought us
possessed of every quality to render him happy, surely
merits our gratitude. If his character is good — if he
is not displeasing in his person or manners — what
objection can we make that will not be thought frivo-

lous by the greater part of the world? — yet I think
there are many other things necessary for happiness,
and the world should never compel me to marry a man
because I could not give satisfactory reasons for not
liking him.   I do not esteem marriage absolutely essential to happiness, and that it does not always bring
happiness we must every day witness in our acquaintance.   A single life is considered too generally as a
reproach; but let me ask you, which is the most despi-
cable — she who marries a man she scarcely thinks *well*
of — to avoid the reputation of an old maid — or she,
who with more delicacy, than marry one she could not
highly esteem, preferred to live single all her life, and
had wisdom enough to despise so mean a sacrifice, to
the opinion of the rabble, as the woman who marries a
man she has not much love for — must make.   I wish
not to alter the làws of nature — neither will I quarrel
with the rules which custom has established and rendered indispensably necessary to the harmony of society.   But every being who has contemplated human
nature on a large scale will certainly justify me when I
declare that the inequality of privilege between the
sexes is very sensibly felt by us females, and in no
instance is it greater than in the liberty of choosing a
partner in marriage; true, we have the liberty of refusing those we don't like, but not of selecting those
we do.   This is undoubtedly as it should be.   But let
me ask you, what must be that love which is altogether voluntary, which we can withhold or give, which

sleeps in dulness and apathy till it is requested to brighten into life? Is it not a cold, lifeless dictate of the head, — do we not weigh all the conveniences and inconveniences which will attend it? And after a long calculation, in which the heart never was consulted, we determine whether it is most prudent to love or not.

How I should despise a soul so sordid, so mean! How I abhor the heart which is regulated by mechanical rules, which can say "thus far will I go and no farther," whose feelings can keep pace with their convenience, and be awakened at stated periods, — a mere piece of clockwork which always moves right! How far less valuable than that being who has a soul to govern her actions, and though she may not always be coldly prudent, yet she will sometimes be generous and noble, and that the other never can be. After all, I must own that a woman of delicacy never will suffer her esteem to ripen into love unless she is convinced of a return. Though our first approaches to love may be involuntary, yet I should be sorry if we had no power of controlling them if occasion required. There is a happy conformity or pliability in the female mind which seems to have been a gift of nature to enable them to be happy with so few privileges, — and another thing, they have more gratitude in their dispositions than men, and there is a something particularly gratifying to the heart in being beloved, if the object is worthy; it produces a something like, and "Pity melts the heart to love." Added to these there is a self-love which does more than all the rest. Our vanity ('tis an ugly word but I can't find a better) is gratified by the distinguished preference given us. There must be an essential difference in the dispositions of men and women. I am astonished when I think of it — yet — But I have written myself into sunshine — 'tis always my way when anything oppresses me, when any chain of thoughts particularly occupies my mind, and I feel dissatisfied at anything which I have not the power to alter, — to sit down and unburthen them on paper; it never fails to alleviate me, and I generally give full scope to the feelings of the moment, and as I write all disagreeable thoughts evaporate, and I end contented that things shall remain as they are. When I began this it absolutely appeared to me that no woman, or rather not one in a hundred, married the man she should prefer to all the world — not that I ever could suppose that at the time she married him she did not prefer him to all others, — but that she would have preferred another if he had professed to love her as well as the one she married. Indeed, I believe no woman of delicacy suffers herself to think she could love any one before she had discovered an affection for her. For my part I should never ask the question of myself — do I love such a one, if I had reason to think he loved me — and I believe there are many who love that never confessed it to themselves. My Pride, my delicacy, would all be hurt if I discovered such *unasked* for love,

even in my own bosom. I would strain every nerve
and rouse every faculty to quell the first appearance of
it. There is no danger, however. I could never love
without being beloved, and I am confident in my own
mind that no person whom I could love would ever
think me sufficiently worthy to love me. But I congratulate myself that I am at liberty to refuse those I
don't like, and that I have firmness enough to brave the
sneers of the world and live an old maid, if I never find
one I can love.

Scarborough, Tuesday Night.

Dear Mother:

We have got Miranda[1] all fix't, only her clothes to
be washed, or rather ironed. You have undoubtedly
got all things ready for her, or you would not send for
her immediately. I suppose we shall send her over in
the stage, as the riding is as yet too bad to go in a
chaise; she wants some pocket handkerchiefs and a
pair of cotton gloves to wear to school; she had 3 pairs
of white mitts and I have given her another pair. I
think she must have another dimity skirt; her jaconet
muslin we could not fix, for it wants a new waist and
sleeves and a hem put on the bottom, and we could get

---

[1] Miranda and Arixene Southgate were at this time aged respectively
twelve and eight years. Their cousin Sally Leland was about the same
age. Frederic Southgate, born in 1791, became a tutor in Bowdoin College, and died unmarried in 1820.

no muslin to pattern it ; you can buy a piece and it can
be sent over any time, she won't need it immediately.
Charles says you told him I must send over to you for
anything I needed.   I want nothing so much as some
new linen and some English stockings ; excepting the
two fine pairs I have none but homespun ones.   I should
like a half dozen pair, 4 at least.   If you see anything
that would be light and handsome for our summer
gowns, I should like you would get them.   Why can't
you go and see McLellan's lace shades?   Perhaps he
may let you have one reasonably.   I think there are
some for 10, 6 and 12 shillings a yard, at 18 they would
not come to more than 9 or 10 dollars ; you can look
at them at least.   I should like one very much.   Sally
Weeks has taken one of them.   We do very well here,
all goes on charmingly, only Arixene loses her thimble,
her needle and anything to avoid working.   Sally Leland has been here ever since Miranda returned, and you
know when they are together there must be romping,
— however, Frederic has gone to carry her home to-day.
Miranda must have my little trunk.   Octavia and I
both want little trunks, my old one is a good size.   How
is Sister? give my love to her, kiss the children ; I really
miss them, and our own don't seem more natural than
they did.   The little *Isabella* [1] (so they say it is) is Aunt
Eliza's darling.   I love that little thing dearly.   I never

[1] *Isabella Boyd*, second child of Isabella Southgate and Joseph Coffin
Boyd. She died of consumption, the fatal disease which carried off so
many of her aunts, sisters, and cousins.

RUFUS KING

From a painting by Woods

loved an infant more in my life, Isabella says it is because it has blue eyes ; she *will* make me selfish. I had
a letter from Martha yesterday, the third since you have
been in Portland ; she mentions Uncle Rufus [1] and family
in all of them. In her last but one she says Aunt King [2]
was confined ; she had dined there the Sunday before,
and they requested her in a billet to bring yours and my
Father's profiles,[3] which I gave her some time before she
went away. She carried them, and Uncle thought them
good likenesses. She admires Uncle Rufus ; she says
when he first called on her he stayed two hours, but she
could have talked with him *two* days. In her last she
says she was to have been introduced at court, but Aunt
King's confinement prevented ; as soon as she gets out
she is to be introduced. She says she shall write by the
Minerva and send the fashions to me. Mr. Smith the
Russian was here last week, bro't me some letters. I
am now writing to Martha, to send by William Weeks ;
'twill be a fine opportunity, and I shall write as much
as I can ; he will probably see her. Mrs. Coffin will be

[1] *Rufus King*, oldest son of Richard King and Isabella Bragdon, and
brother of Mrs. Southgate. He was born in 1755 and married Mary
Alsop. He was delegated by the State of Massachusetts to the Conven-
tion for framing the Constitution of the United States, was a member of
Congress from Massachusetts, Senator of the United States from New
York, and at this time Minister to the Court of St. James.

[2] *Mary Alsop* was born in 1786. She was the daughter of John Alsop
and Mary Frogat.

[3] Mr. and Mrs. Southgate's "profiles" hung in Mr. King's house at
Jamaica until about 1875, when they were given by his granddaughter to
Mrs. Southgate's grandson, Mr. Lawrence, of Flushing, L. I.

delighted with such an opportunity. Don't hurry home until you have staid as long as you wish, for I don't know anything at present that requires your presence. I think I make a very good manager, and tell Sister Boyd I am astonished to find how I have improved in my housewife talents this last winter. The children won't allow me absolute rule among them, but I have the worst of it; they do pretty well, considering what a young gay mistress they have. I sometimes get up to dance and all of them flock up to help me, and when I am tired I find it difficult to still them, so as I set the example I am obliged to put up with it. I have not been out of the yard since I came home till this afternoon. I rode a mile or two on horseback just to smell the fresh air. I never was more contented in my life; tho' I have not seen anybody but Mr. Smith these 3 weeks almost, I have not had an hour hang heavily on me; 'tis charming to get home after being gone so long! I believe you will think I am never going to leave off.

Your affectionate   ELIZA.

To Mrs. Mary King Southgate, Portland.

Portland, March 18, 1801.

Thank you for being so particular in your description of your eastern tour. I told you that Wiscassett would delight you; ease and sociability you know always please you. By the bye, Jewett thought *Saco* was the land of milk and honey, such fine buxom girls! so easy and familiar. Dorcas Stour charmed him much, her haughty forbidding manners corresponded with the dignity of her sentiments, so he says, something congenial in their dispositions I think. But he has made his selection — Miss Weeks is handsome, censorious, animated, violent in her prejudices, genteel, impatient of contradiction, speaks her sentiments very freely, has many admirers and many enemies, — on the whole a pleasant companion amongst friends. — How think they will do together? Jewett you know.

Last evening I was out at Broads;[1] we had only 7 in our party— a very pleasant one. Jewett, Horatio, William Weeks, and Charles Little were our beaux. Miss Weeks, Miss Boardman (from Exeter), and myself, the ladies. Mr. Little is engaged to Miss Boardman; he is an open, honest, unaffected, plain, *clever* fellow. She has a pleasant face, an open guileless heart, plain unaffected manners, a clumsy shape, easy in company — but it is rather the ease which a calm, even temper produces, than that which is acquired in polite circles. I think they are as much alike as possible and 'twill be a pleasant couple. We played cards, talked and wrote crambo; after we had scribbled the backs of two packs of cards, cut half of them up, and eat our supper, we set out for home, about one o'clock. You say in your last that if reports are true, I am on the highway to matrimony, — you know what I always said with regard to these things; if they are true, well and good — if they are not, let them take their course, they will be short-

---

[1] *Broads*, a tavern near Portland, to which gay parties of young people went on frolics.

lived.   I despise the conduct of those girls who think
that every man who pays them any attention is seriously
in love with them, and begin to bridle up, look conscious,
fearful lest every word the poor fellow utters should be
a declaration of love.   I have no idea that every gentleman that has a particular partiality for a lady thinks
seriously of being connected with her, and I think any
lady puts herself in a most awkward situation to appear
in constant fear or expectation that the gentleman is
going to make love to her.   I despise coquetry, — every
lady says the same, you will say, — but if I know myself
at all — my heart readily assents to its truth — I think
no lady has a right to encourage hopes that she means
never to gratify, but I think she is much to blame if she
considers these little attentions as a proof of love; they
often mean nothing, and should be treated as such.
The gentleman in question I own pays me more attention than any other gentleman, yet I say sincerely, I
don't think he means any thing more than to please his
fancy for the present.   I pride myself upon my sincerity,
and if I ever am engaged, I trust it will be to one whom
I shall not be ashamed to acknowledge.   Our intimacy
has been of long standing.   He and Enoch Jones were
Martha's most intimate acquaintance, they were there
almost every evening.   Here comes Enoch and William
[Weeks], we used to say as soon as we heard the knocker
in the evening.   I was always at the Doctor's a great
part of the time I spent in Portland, I could not but be
intimate with them.   I liked them both, they were pleasant companions, and I was always glad to see them come

in ; — since that time, Enoch has been gone most of the
time, and William has been left alone ; — true, he has this
winter been more attentive to me than usual ; he lent
me books, drawings, and music ; he used often to be my
gallant home from parties if I walked, and if I rode help
me to the sleigh, yet every gentleman does the same, —
all have a favorite, some for a month, some a little longer.
It seems like making you a confidant to talk thus, but I
say many things which would appear ridiculous if com-
municated to a third person, and I know you would have
too much delicacy to communicate any thing which
might hurt my feelings. I have heard all these stories
before, yet I must act and judge for myself. I know
better than any other person can, how far they are true,
and I candidly confess that he never said a word to me
which I could possibly construe into a declaration of
love, not the most faint or distant. Then think for a
moment how ridiculous it would be for me to alter my
conduct towards him ! No ! while he treats me as a
friend, I shall treat him as such ; and let the world say
what they will, I will endeavor to act in a manner that
my conscience will justify, — to steer between the rocks
of prudery and coquetry, and take my own sense of propriety as a pilot that will conduct me safe. I should
not have been thus particular, but I felt unwilling that
you should be led into error that I could easily remove
from your mind ; it would seem like giving a silent
assent, as I confess to write as I think to you, and to
speak openly on all occasions, I felt that I ought to say
more to you on this affair than I ever have to any other.

Let the world still have it as they will. I confess it would be more pleasing to me if my name was not so much [1] . . . what Johnson says of an author may apply . . . is much known in the world. That his name like . . . must be beat backward and forward as it falls to the ground. I recollect in a former letter you asked why I did not say more of particular characters, and among my acquaintance select some and give you a few characteristic sketches. The truth is — I felt afraid to, I did not know but you might mention many things which would make me enemies. I am always willing to speak my opinion without reserve on any character, because I should take care that I spoke it before those who would not abuse the frankness; but letters may be miscarried, may fall into hands we know not of, — but I never think of these, or I am sure I should burn this in a moment, — another thing that it requires a quiet discernment, a correct judgment and a thorough knowledge of the world, of human nature, to form a just character of any one that we are not intimately acquainted with. However, we all of us form an opinion of every person we see, and whatever I shall say and have said you must recollect is only the opinion of one who is oftener wrong than right, and you can form no correct idea of my character from what I say.

Scarborough, March, Sunday.

P. S. — Congratulate me, I am at home at last! Come and see us, — we expect Miss Tappan to-morrow

---

[1] The manuscript which was under the seal was so torn as to make this sentence illegible.

and Paulina Porter [1] and Miranda Southgate. I wish much to see Miss T. I think I shall like her ; tell her she does not know what she lost last week, — a young gentleman came several miles out of his way only to see her; she was not here and he returned to Portland with a heavy heart. Jewett says she is rather shy.

I meant to have written more about Wiscassett, about Miss R.,[2] but I must leave that for another letter. I have a great deal to say on that head, — "exercise the same coolness and judgment as in choosing a horse !" I heard a gentleman make really the same observation, and yet that very gentleman is raving, distractedly in love, — he is a little calmer now, but he was a madman. He, like you, always talks of his insensibility, his coldness and discretion, and he, like you, is always upon extremes, extravagant beyond all bounds. More hereafter.

Mr. Moses Porter.

---

[1] *Paulina Porter,* daughter of Dr. Aaron Porter of Portland. She married, first Enoch Jones, and then Edward Beecher. Her sister Harriet married Lyman Beecher.

[2] *Miss Rice's* father was Joseph Rice ; he raised a company of fifty men and, after the receipt of the news of the skirmish at Lexington, set out as soon as possible for Cambridge and joined Colonel Phinney's regiment. It was the first regiment that marched into Boston after its evacuation by the British on the 17th of March, 1776. In a letter from Rufus King to Dr. Southgate, dated August 6, 1776, he says : "Phinney's regiment is ordered from Boston to Ticonderoga. I guess the pious Elder would as lieve tarry where he is, but he was formerly fond of action — hope now he will be satisfied. . . . Gen. Gates will doubtless make a stand at Ticonderoga."

Thursday, April 8th.

I have been thinking on that part of your letter which interests me most, respecting the propriety of conduct, opinion of the world, etc., etc. I don't exactly recollect what I wrote in my last, but I am positive you have mistaken my meaning, or at least have taken what I said on too large a scale; — as a general rule of conduct, in so extensive a sense as you talk about, such doctrine would indeed be pernicious. But whatever I said I meant to apply to this particular case, and perhaps did not express myself so clearly as I ought to have done. You have described principles which I have ever condemned — as those I now act upon. Perhaps I shall find it impossible fully to explain my sentiments on this subject — it is of a delicate nature; and many things I shall say will probably bear a misconstruction. However, I trust to your candor to judge with lenity, and to your knowledge of my heart, to believe I would not intentionally deviate from the laws of female delicacy and propriety. Reputation undoubtedly is of great importance to all, but to a female 'tis every thing, — once lost 'tis *forever* lost. Whatever I may have said, my heart too sensibly tells me I have none of that boasted independence of mind which can stand collected in its own worth, and let the censure and malice of the world pass by as the "idle wind which we regard not." I have ever thought that to be conscious of doing right was insufficient; but that it must appear so to

the world. How I could have blundered upon a sentiment which I despise, or how I could have written anything to bear such a construction as you have put upon
a part of my letter, I know not. When I said that I
should let these reports pass off without notice or pre-
tending to vindicate myself, 'twas not because I de-
spised the opinion of the world, but as the most effectual
method to preserve it! — *You* say as well as myself, that
whatever we say in vindication of ourselves, only makes
the matter worse. When I said, that I meant not to
alter my conduct while my conscience did not accuse
me, I had no idea that you would suppose my conduct
towards him had ever been of a kind that required an
alteration, or any thing more pointed than to any other
gentleman. I supposed you would infer from what I
said that it was such as propriety and a regard for my
reputation would sanction. I know not what you think
it has been, but if I can judge of my own actions, —
their motives I know I can, but I mean the outward
appearance, — I have never treated him with any more
distinction than any other gentleman, nor have appeared more pleased with his attentions than with another's ; believe me, I have kept constantly in view the
opinion of the world, and if you knew every circumstance of my life, you would be convinced my feelings
were " tremblingly alive " to all its slanders. But
" something too much of this " ; you, who know my disposition, may easily conceive how often I subject myself to the envenomed shafts of censure and malice, by

that gaiety and high flow of spirits, which I sometimes
think my greatest misfortune to possess, — sometimes
I err in judgment — don't always see the right path, —
sometimes I see it, yet the warmth and ardor of my
feelings force me out of it. Yet in this affair I feel confident I have acted from right principles, — there are
a thousand trifling things which at times influenced my
conduct, which you cannot know, and you may be surprised when I say that his attentions were of a kind
that politeness obliged me to receive, nor should I ever
have suspected they meant any thing more than gallantry and politeness, had not the babbles of the world
put it into my head. You have been misinformed in
many respects, I am convinced. You mentioned his
constant visits at Sister Boyd's. I declare to you he
never was there a half dozen times the three months I
was in Portland, excepting the morning after the assemblies, when the gentlemen all go to see their partners; neither was I his constant partner at assemblies.
I never danced but two dances in an evening with him
all winter, excepting once, and then there was a mistake, — this surely was nothing remarkable, for I always
danced two with Mr. Smith at every assembly we were
at. I danced as much with one as the other. True, he
was my partner at 2 parties at Broads. I at the time
asked Horatio, when he mentioned the party, why he
would not carry me; he said if I was asked by any
other, to say I was going with my brother, would be
considered as a tacit declaration that I had an aversion

to going with him, therefore 'twould have been folly.
You cannot judge unless you know a thousand customs
and every . . . which they have in Portland. But I
declare to you, Cousin, I am much gratified that you
told me what you thought — had you have locked it in
your bosom, I should never have had an opportunity to
vindicate myself. I beg of you always to write with
freedom, always write with the same openness you did
in your last — 'tis one of the greatest advantages I expect to derive from our correspondence — I enjoin it
upon you as you value my happiness. I told you I
would show you some of Martha's letters; I had one
from her since I wrote you, in which she says I must
on no condition whatever show her letters, — however,
I will read you some passages in some of them. You
shall see some parts; I will make my peace with — indeed I know she would not object. I love to show you
her letters because you feel something as I do in reading them. You admire her or you should not be the
friend of   ELIZA.

P. S. I wrote this letter last night intending to keep
it by me to send whenever I please; all the family were
absent, left me reading, — I read your letter, the house
was silent, and I was entirely alone. I knew I should
not have another opportunity as convenient for giving
you my sentiments — no fear of intrusion — and I therefore took my pen and scribbled what I now send you,
but I believe I must adopt your plan and send it im-

mediately to the office, — but I repent and burn it, and
I find on reading it that I have said not half I meant
to ; but I will send it away immediately. I am almost
ashamed to answer yours so soon, 'tis so unlike the
example you set me that I suppose you will say 'tis a
tacit disapprobation of your conduct.

Scarborough, April 9th.

Mr. Moses Porter, Biddeford.

Sunday, Scarborough, May —, 1801.

When one commences an action with a full conviction they shall not acquit themselves with honor, they
are sure not to succeed; imprest with this idea I write
you. I positively declare I have felt a great reluctance
ever since we concluded on the plan. I am aware of
the construction you may put on this, but call it *affectation* or what you will, I assure you it proceeds from different motives. When I first proposed this correspondence, I thought only of the amusement and instruction it would afford *me*. I almost forgot that I should
have any part to perform. Since, however, I have reflected on the scheme as it was about to be carried
into execution, I have felt a degree of diffidence which
has almost induced me to hope you would *forget* the
engagement. Fully convinced of my inability to afford
pleasure or instruction to an enlarged mind, I rely
wholly on your candor and generosity to pardon the
errors which will cloud my best efforts. When I re-

flect on the severity of your criticisms in general, I
shrink at the idea of exposing to you what will never
stand the test. Yet did I not imagine you would throw
aside the *critic* and assume the *friend*, I should never
dare, with all my vanity (and I am not deficient), give
you so fine an opportunity to exercise your favorite propensity. I know you will laugh at all this, and I must
confess it appears rather a folly, first to request your
correspondence and then with so much diffidence and
false delicacy, apparently to extort a compliment, talk
about my inability and the like. You will not think I
intend a compliment when I say I have ever felt a disagreeable restraint when conversing before you. Often,
when with all the confidence I possess I have brought
forward an opinion, said all my imagination could sug-
gest in support of it, and viewed with pleasure the little
fabric, which I imagined to be founded on truth and
justice, with one word you would crush to the ground
that which had cost me so many to erect. These things
I think in time will humble my vanity, I wish sincerely
that they may.

Yet I believe I possess decent talents and should
have been quite another being had they been properly
cultivated. But as it is, I can never get over some little prejudices which I have imbibed long since, and
which warp all the faculties of my mind. I was pushed
on to the stage of action without one principle to guide
my actions, — the impulse of the moment was the only
incitement. I have never committed any grossly im-

prudent action, yet I have been folly's darling child.   I
trust they were rather errors of the head than the
heart, for we have all a kind of inherent power to distinguish between right and wrong, and if before the
heart becomes contaminated by the maxims of society
it is left to act from impulse though it have no fixt
principle, yet it will not materially err.   Possessing a
gay lively disposition, I pursued pleasure with ardor.   I
wished for admiration, and took the means which would
be most likely to obtain it.   I found the mind of a
female, if such a thing existed, was thought not worth
cultivating.   I disliked the trouble of thinking for myself and therefore adopted the sentiments of others —
fully convinced to adorn my person and acquire a few
little accomplishments was sufficient to secure me the
admiration of the society I frequented.   I cared but
little about the mind.   I learned to flutter about with
a thoughtless gaiety — a mere feather which every
breath had power to move.   I left school with a head
full of something, tumbled in without order or connection.   I returned home with a determination to put it
in more order ; I set about the great work of culling the
best part to make a few sentiments out of — to serve as
a little ready change in my commerce with the world.
But I soon lost all patience (a virtue I do not possess
in an eminent degree), for the greater part of my ideas
I was obliged to throw away without knowing where I
got them or what I should do with them ; what remained
I pieced as ingeniously as I could into a few patchwork

opinions, — they are now almost worn threadbare, and as I am about quilting a few more, I beg you will send me any spare ideas you may chance to have that will answer my turn. By this time I suppose you have found out what you have a right to expect from this correspondence, and probably at this moment lay down the letter with a long sage-like face to ponder on my egotism. — 'Tis a delightful employment, I will leave you to enjoy it while I eat my dinner : And what is the result, Cousin ? I suppose a few exclamations on the girl's vanity to think no subject could interest me but where herself was concerned, or the barrenness of her head that could write on no other subject. But she is a *female*, say you, with a *manly contempt.* Oh you Lords of the world, what are you that your unhallowed lips should dare profane the fairest part of creation ! But honestly I wish to say something by way of apology, but don't seem to know what, — it is true I have a kind of natural affection for myself, I find no one more ready to pardon my faults or find excuses for my failings — it is natural to love our friends.

I have positively not said one single thing which I intended when I sat down ; my motive was to answer your letter, and I have not mentioned my not having received it ? — Your opinion of Story's Poems I think very unjust ; as to the *man*, I cannot say, for I know nothing of him, but I think you are too severe upon him ; a man who had not a "fibre of refinement in his composition" could never have written some passages in that poem.

What is refinement? I thought it was a delicacy of taste which might be acquired, if not any thing in our nature, — true, there are some so organized that they are incapable of receiving a delicate impression, but we won't say any thing of such beings. I just begin to feel in a mood for answering your letter. What you say of Miss Rice — I hardly know how to refuse the challenge; she possesses no quality above mediocrity, and yet is just what a female ought to be. Now what I would give for a little *Logic*, or for a little skill to support an argument. But I give it up, for tho' you might not convince me, you would *confound* me with so many *learned* observations that my vanity would oblige me to say I was convinced to prevent the mortification of saying I did not understand you. How did you like Mr. Coffin? Write soon and tell me. We expect you to go to the fishing party with us on Tuesday. Mr. Coffin told us you would all come. You must be here by 9 o'clock (not before) (in the morning). My love to the girls, and tell them — no! I'll tell them myself.

ELIZA.

To Mr. Moses Porter, Biddeford.

Scarborough, June 1st, 1801.

As to the qualities of mind peculiar to each sex, I agree with you that sprightliness is in favor of females and profundity of males. Their education, their pursuits would create such a quality even tho' nature had not implanted it. The business and pursuits of men require deep thinking, judgment, and moderation, while, on the other hand, females are under no necessity of dipping deep, but merely "skim the surface," and we too commonly spare ourselves the exertion which deep researches require, unless they are absolutely necessary to our pursuits in life. We rarely find one giving themselves up to profound investigation for amusement merely. Necessity is the nurse of all the great qualities of the mind; it explores all the hidden treasures and by its stimulating power they are "polished into brightness." Women who have no such incentives to action suffer all the strong energetic qualities of the mind to sleep in obscurity ; sometimes a ray of genius gleams through the thick clouds with which it is enveloped, and irradiates for a moment the darkness of mental night ; yet, like a comet that shoots wildly from its sphere, it excites our wonder, and we place it among the phenomenons of nature, without searching for a natural cause. Thus it is the qualities with which nature has endowed us, as a support amid the misfortunes of life and a shield from the allurements of vice, are left to moulder in ruin. In this dormant state they become enervated and impaired, and at last die for *want of exercise.* The little airy qualities which produce sprightliness are left to flutter about like feathers in the wind, the sport of every breeze.

Women have more fancy, more lively imaginations than men. That is easily accounted for : a person of

correct judgment and accurate discernment will never
have that flow of ideas which one of a different character might, — every object has not the power to introduce into his mind such a variety of ideas, he rejects
all but those closely connected with it. On the other
hand, a person of small discernment will receive every
idea that arises in the mind, making no distinction between those nearly related and those more distant, they
are all equally welcome, and consequently such a mind
abounds with fanciful, out-of-the-way ideas. Women
have more imagination, more sprightliness, because
they have less discernment. I never was of opinion
that the pursuits of the sexes ought to be the same; on
the contrary, I believe it would be destructive to happiness, there would a degree of rivalry exist, incompatible
with the harmony we wish to establish. I have ever
thought it necessary that each should have a separate
sphere of action, — in such a case there could be no
clashing unless one or the other should leap their re-
spective bounds. Yet to cultivate the qualities with
which we are endowed can never be called infringing
the prerogatives of man. Why, my dear Cousin, were
we furnished with such powers, unless the improvement
of them would conduce to the happiness of society?
Do you suppose the mind of woman the only work of
God that was "made in vain." The cultivation of the
powers we possess, I have ever thought a privilege (or
I may say duty) that belonged to the human species,
and not man's exclusive prerogative. Far from de-

stroying the harmony that ought to subsist, it would fix
it on a foundation that would not totter at every jar.
Women would be under the same degree of subordina-
tion that they now are; enlighten and expand their
minds, and they would perceive the necessity of such a
regulation to preserve the order and happiness of society. Yet you require that their conduct should be
always guided by that reason which you refuse them
the power of exercising. I know it is generally thought
that in such a case women would assume the right of
commanding. But I see no foundation for such a
supposition, — not a blind submission to the will of
another which neither honor nor reason dictates. It
would be criminal in such a case to submit, for we are
under a prior engagement to conduct in all things according to the dictates of reason. I had rather be the
meanest reptile that creeps the earth, or cast upon
the wide world to suffer all the ills " that flesh is heir
to," than live a slave to the despotic will of another.

I am aware of the censure that will ever await the
female that attempts the vindication of her sex, yet I
dare to brave that censure that I know to be unde-
served. It does not follow (O what a pen !) that every
female who vindicates the capacity of the sex is a disci-
ple of Mary Wolstoncraft. Though I allow her to have
said many things which I cannot but approve, yet the
very foundation on which she builds her work will be
apt to prejudice us so against her that we will not allow
her the merit she really deserves, — yet, prejudice set

aside, I confess I admire many of her sentiments, not-withstanding I believe should any one adopt her prin-ciples, they would conduct in the same manner, and upon the whole her life is the best comment on her writings. Her style is nervous and commanding, her sentiments appear to carry conviction along with them, but they will not bear analyzing. I wish to say some-thing on your *natural refinement*, but I shall only have room to touch upon it if I begin, "therefore I'll leave it till another time."

Last evening Mr. Samuel Thatcher spent with us; we had a fine "dish of conversation" served up with great taste, fine sentiments dressed with elegant lan-guage and seasoned with wit. He is really excellent company — a little enthusiastic or so — but that is no matter. In compassion I entreat you to come over here soon and make me some pens. I have got one that I have been whittling this hour and at last have got it to make a stroke (it liked to have given me the lie). I believe I must give up all pretension to *profun-dity*, for I am much more at home in my female char-acter. This argumentative style is not congenial to my taste. I hate anything that requires order or con-nection. I never could do anything by rule, — when I get a subject I am incapable of reasoning upon, I play with it as with a rattle, for what else should I do with it? But I have kept along quite in a direct line; I caught myself "upon the wing" two or three times, but I had power to check my nonsense. I send you my sentiments on this subject as they really exist with me. I believe they are not the mere impulse of the moment, but founded on what I think truth. I could not help laughing at that part of your letter where you said the seal of my letter deprived you of some of the most interesting part of it. I declare positively I left a blank place on purpose for it, that you might not lose one precious word, and now you have the impudence to tell me that the most interesting part was the blank paper. It has provoked my ire to such a degree that I positively declare I never will send you any more blank paper than I possibly can avoid, to "spite you."

To Mr. Moses Porter. E. S.

Portland, July 17, 1801.

I almost at this moment wish myself in your situation, meeting old acquaintances, shaking hands with old friends and telling over with renewed pleasure your College frolicks. I can almost see you convulsed with laughter, hear you recount the adventures of the last year, while imagination brings every boyish frolic to your view, unimpaired by time. What a world of humour! what flashes of wit! what animated descriptions! O these social meetings! How they animate and inspire one! how they lighten the cares and multiply the joys of life! I wish you would write me about Commencement. I heard yesterday that Sam. Fay of Concord delivered an oration the 4th of July. I should admire to see it.   I know it must be very fine; in my opinion he is a man of excellent talents, capable of writing on the occasion an oration that would reflect great honor.   The sentiments must be noble and generous. He possesses so much feeling, there must be many glowing passages in it.   If it is possible I beg you will get me a copy and I will confess myself very, very greatly obliged.   Last night I attended the *Theater*, — "Speed the plough" was performed, and I assure you very *decently;* the characters in general were well supported.   Villiers in Fannie Ashfield really outdid himself; he threw off the monkey and became a good honest clown, and did not, as he usually does, outstep the bounds of nature and all other bounds.   Mrs. Powell as Miss Blandford delighted us all.   How I admire that woman!   She is perfectly at home on the stage, and yet there is no levity in her appearance; she has great energy, acts with spirit, with feeling, yet never rants; her private character we all know is unexceptionable.   Mr. Donnee as a young buck is very pleasing, he has a most melodious voice in speaking, and has a very easy, stylish air, — good figure, tho' small.   As for Mrs. Harper she is my aversion — for, as Shakespeare says, she will "tear a passion to tatters, to very rags," and she is too indecent ever to appear on the stage.   Harper is a fine fellow; he appears best among the common herd of Players, and has as much judgment in supporting his part as any one I ever saw, and even in comic characters I think he excels Villiers.   He has much greater resources within himself. Villiers gains applause by distorting his face and playing the monkey, while Harper adheres more strictly to nature. In Villiers we cannot help seeing the player thro' the thin disguise, — *Villiers*, not the character he personates, is continually in our minds. S. Powell is contemptible as a player (and I believe as a man) ; he puffs and blows so incessantly that it is enough to put one into a fever to see him ; he does not know in the least how to preserve a medium, but takes a certain pitch and there remains ; he cannot gradually bring his passion to the height, but he thunders it out without any preparation, and the unvarying monotony of his voice is truly disgusting. I am sure, by his strutting and bellowing, Hamlet would think *he* was made by one of "Nature's journeymen." But it is time to have done with players, for you will think my head turned indeed if I rant about them any longer ; but it has served to fill up a part of my letter, and I assure you that alone was a sufficient reason why I should give them a place. Society, bustle, and noise frustrate all my ideas. I cannot write anywhere but at home. I am ashamed that things of so little consequence should turn my head, but 'tis a melancholy truth. O you malicious fellow, don't talk to me about my favorite topic "female education," don't tell me of your *philosophical indifference!* O Moses, you can't leave the subject, every word that could any way dash at it is marked. I believe you do *itch* to commence the attack. Well, rail on, you shall not say it is in compassion to me that you desist. God forbid that your greatest enemy should ever inflict so severe a punishment as to prohibit you from speaking of your "favorite topic." I fancy you have forgotten that it *is* such, *Mr. Indifference.* Your ironical letter has had a wonderful effect, but perhaps not the desired one. I blush not to confess myself contemptibly inferior to my antagonist. You ought to blush, but from a very different cause ; but I had forgotten myself, and was taking the thing too seriously. I am not slow at taking the hint, perhaps my presumption merited the reproof. I receive it and will endeavor to profit by it ; and pray, Cousin, how does Mr. Symmes' coat suit you ? His " haughty humility," his "condescending pride." You have assumed the habit, and I hope will ever clothe yourself with it when you meet your *superior antagonist.*

You have a fine imagination and have pictured a chain of delightful events which probably will exist there alone, yet I should have no objection to your being a true prophet. We all can plan delightful schemes, but they rarely ever become realities ; but no matter, we enjoy them in imagination. I expect from you a particular account of yourself when you return. You will have many amusing anecdotes to tell me, if you will take the trouble. I have just read your last and picture something in it that at first I did not pay much attention to. You say all you have said on the subject of education was merely the thought of the moment, "written not to be received but laughed at." What shall I think ? — That you think me too contemptible to know your real sentiments ? I should be very unwilling to admit such a suspicion, yet what can you mean ? — with the greatest apparent seriousness, you speak of the *sincerity* with which you conduct this correspondence. Was that likewise meant to be laughed at? I had flattered myself, when I commenced this correspondence, to reap both instruction and amusement from an undisguised communication of sentiments. I had likewise hoped you would not think it too great a condescension to speak to me with that openness you would to a male friend. However, I shall begin to think it is contrary to the nature of things that a gentleman should speak his real sentiments to a lady, yet in our correspondence I wished and expected to step aside from the world, speak to each other in the plain language of sincerity. I have much to say on this subject, but unfortunately my ideas never begin to flow until I have filled up my paper. Do not imagine from what I have said that the most disagreeable truths will offend me. I promise not to feel hurt at any thing you write, if 'tis your real sentiment. But, Cousin, don't trifle with me. Do not make me think so contemptibly of myself as you will by not allowing me your confidence; promise to speak as you think and I will never scold you again.   Eliza.

Cousin, I wish you would write a list of your mother's children, names and ages, those that have died together with the others. We are going to send them out to Uncle Rufus, as he requested it some time since. By Martha it will be a fine opportunity, — as soon as convenient send them over.

Mr. Moses Porter,
     Biddeford.

Scarborough, August 6, 1801.

Hon. Rufus King.

Pardon, my dear Sir, the liberty I take in addressing you, and let my motives shield me from the imputation of presumption. Some time since, you requested a list of my Aunt Porter's and our family. It has never been sent, and as we have now a very favorable opportunity, my father has requested me to make it out and enclose it to you. I tremble while I write, lest I should appear disrespectful in my manner of addressing you. Unused as I am to writing to any one so much superior in years, I cannot but feel embarrassed. A degree of confidence in ourselves is necessary in every undertaking to ensure success ; as I feel at this moment destitute of that confidence, I likewise despair of succeeding in my wishes, yet I entreat you to attribute whatever may appear assuming rather to an incapacity of expressing myself as I wish than to a want of respect. When I consider you as a public character esteemed and respected by your country, I would willingly shrink from observation, lest my intruding myself on your attention should be thought impertinence. But when I think how nearly I am allied, I flatter myself I shall obtain that indulgence which I now earnestly solicit. Mr. and Mrs. Derby, by whom I shall send this, intend taking the tour of Europe after having taken that of the United States. Mrs. Derby is my particular friend, and as she is intimately acquainted in our family, can give you whatever information you

Mrs. RUFUS KING

After a portrait by Trumbull.

ARTOTYPE, E. BIERSTADT, N. Y.

wish respecting us. I say nothing to remind her, for I
have too high an opinion of your discernment to suppose
any recommendation necessary. My mother joins me
in desiring you would make our respects acceptable to
Mrs. King, and all the family unite in earnest wishes for
the complete restoration of her health. Our family are
all in good health . . . My mother really looks young!
My Aunt Porter [Pauline] is not wholly restored to her
former health, but is much better than she has been for
many years past.

I cannot conclude this without earnestly intreating
you to receive it with the candor of an Uncle rather
than the severity of a critic. I feel I do not write as I
ought to, yet I entreat you not to think me deficient in
that respect and esteem with which I shall ever remain

Your niece   ELIZA SOUTHGATE.

Scarborough, August 4, 1801.

Dr. Southgate to Rufus King in London.

You will receive this by Mr. Richard Derby, youngest
son of the late H. Derby of Salem. His lady who ac-
companies him is the daughter of Dr. N. Coffin of Portland. The Doctor's family and mine have ever been on
terms of intimacy and friendship. Mrs. Derby in particular has ever been a favorite of my daughters Octavia and Eliza. They can give you all particulars about
friends at home.

Bath, Sunday, Sept. 13.

There are some kinds of indisposition that instead of weakening the faculties of the mind, serve only to render them more vigorous and sprightly, and in proportion as the body is debilitated, the mind is strengthened. I have every reason to believe that the imagination never soars to such lofty heights as it sometimes does in sickness. But where am I ! What about — Well may *you* ask the question. Believe me, Cousin, I have attempted to finish this letter 4 times this day. I cannot account for my inability to write. It used to be the joy of my life, nothing delighted me so much as to steal into the chamber by myself and scribble an hour, but since I received your last I have often attempted to answer it, but in vain. I have a stubborn brain ; it must be coaxed, not driven. I find there is nothing so tedious as to write when we are not in the mood for it. You may easily see that I am not in one at present. Now for Heaven's sake see what I have written — find the chain that connects. When I began I meant to say I had been quite unwell ever since I left Portland, that some disorders only served to give vigor to the mind, &c., &c., but I *meant* also to say mine was altogether of a different nature. But as I left that out, so I had better have done the other. Oh — 'tis too, too bad ! I'll not write another till I think I can understand it after it is written. I am low-spirited, stupid and everything else.

Now I shall really think I have no *soul* if I find myself as destitute of ideas as I was on Sunday. I have
just been viewing the most delightful prospect I have
seen this long time, and if it has left no more impression
on my mind than objects passing before a mirror, I shall
think myself devoid of every quality that constitutes us
rational beings. I think nature has done everything to
render Bath pleasant : the window at which I now sit
commands a most delightful water prospect ; the river
is about a mile in breadth at this place, the opposite
banks are neither sublime nor beautiful. What if I for a
moment should take a poet's license, and by the force of
imagination project steep and rugged rocks ! bid them
stoop with awful majesty to reflect their gloomy horrors
in the wave ! See you not that enormous precipice
whose awful summit was ne'er profaned by human foot-
steps ? Does not your blood freeze as it creeps along
your veins ? Behold again that barren waste, the axe
nor the plough have never clothed it with a borrowed
charm, or robbed it of those nature bestowed upon it ;
it still boasts its independence of the labor of man.
But to leave fiction for reality, the surface of the water
is a perfect mirror. I never saw it so perfectly smooth ;
at this moment there is a boat passing, rowed by two
men — the reflection in the water is so distinct, so very
clear, it looks like two boats. I admire to see a boat
rowed; it seems to look like arms or wings, moving with

graceful majesty, while the boat cuts the liquid bosom of the water, leaving as it recedes a widening track. There is always to me something very charming in the rowing of a boat. There is music in the motion; and what can be more graceful and majestic than the motion of a *ship under sail?* Yesterday there was a *brig* passed by here — 'twas within hearing — very near. I never was more forcibly struck than at the moment; I longed to prostrate myself in humble admiration — as she approached with a slow, commanding, *celestial* air; — at the moment I am sure it gave me a better idea of the awful grandeur of a deity than anything I had ever seen. I saw Juno's dignified gracefulness such as I had read of but could not conceive.

I have often in reading been disagreeably struck by the epithets used for the motions of the gods. Sometimes they make them *glide* thro' the air, sometimes approach with a solemn *step*, and many other words I do not recollect; nor do I at present think of any words that would answer better — yet *to glide* seems stealing along — to move rapidly and imperceptibly; — a bird glides thro' the air, yet there is nothing celestial in the flight of a bird. It seems to me properly applied to *fairies;* something light and airy should glide, — that a fairy should glide along seems right, — just as I have an idea of them. And then for a god *to step* — that seems too grovelling, too like us mortals, — yet that in my opinion is better than the other.

The place on which this house stands seems to pro-

ject in a small degree toward the water. I believe there
is not a window in the house that does not command a
view of the water. In front there is a kind of cove the
water makes in several rods; the river is broad and
straight, the land rises gradually from it a half mile; —
but I think it is to be regretted that the inhabitants
have built under the *hill,* or rather that they did not
prefer climbing a little higher; however, I think it
must have a fine appearance from the water. Last year
I recollect sailing along in front of the settlement and
remarked how much more compact it looked than it
really is, the houses rising one above the other in such
a manner that every one was seen distinctly. I think
nothing can be more beautiful than a town built on a
sloping ground ascending from so fine a river as this
branch of the Kennebec. All the navigation belonging
to the different ports on this river above Bath, passes
directly by here, and several times I have seen 12 or
14 at a time. To one who has been brought up amidst
salt marsh and flats, this large fine river affords much
novelty and amusement, and I cannot confess but the
sensations I feel in viewing it are more pleasing than
those produced by a stagnant water in a Scarborough
salt pond. I have almost filled my sheet without saying a word of your letter, indeed I have forgotten what
was in it — at the time you gave it me I know I received
it with much pleasure, as it robbed me of some painful
moments. After Horatio's recovery I sat down one
evening to write you, but I had only written the day of

the month, when a most violent clap of thunder (the same that struck Mrs. Horper's house) shook the pen from my hand and my desk from my lap. I do not imagine even by this omen that I offend the strictest laws of virtue and propriety by continuing to write you, therefore should something equally powerful wrest the pen from my hand, depend upon it I will seize it with renewed vigor and dare assure you of my esteem, &c., &c. ELIZA.

I shall go to Wiscassett on Monday; expect to hear from me after I return to Bath; while there I shall have no time. I expect to have important communications to forward — a certain pair of sparkling eyes, which are far more eloquent than her tongue! Now I have half a mind to be affronted. I know at this time, as soon as you have read this you are tumbling it into your pocket as waste paper to ponder on the brilliancy of said eyes. Is it true? Well, I shall see them soon and shall be tempted to ask some atonement for the damages I may suffer. Write me often while I am here, it is your *duty*.

Mr. Moses Porter, Biddeford.

By Mrs. King.

To Mr. Moses Porter at Biddeford.

I want to write, yet I don't want to write to you, my *ceremonious* Cousin, but at this time I can think of nobody else and am *compelled* to address you. My last was dated from Bath, so is this; since then I have made

a visit to Wiscassett. Oh I believe — yes I did write a
few lines from there by Uncle Thatcher — I had forgotten that I wrote any more than the letter I finished
before I left Bath. I wish I could give you an account
of my spending my fortnight at Wiscasset, which would
amuse you as much as the reality did me, but that is
impossible. I have seen so many new faces — (I was
going to say new characters, but they were generally
such as we see every day), so many handsome ladies,
so many fine men, indeed I have seen a little of everything. Mr. Wild and Mr. Davis (of Portland) kept at
Mrs. Lee's. Mr. Wild is a most charming man, and
sensible and genteel, apparently has one of the mildest
and most amiable dispositions in the world. Mr. Davis
you know. There was a Miss P—— spent 2 or 3 days
at Mrs. Lee's. She was — was — I can't tell you what;
you may have heard of her, celebrated for her wit, lost
a lover by exercising it rather too severely; poor soul!
it was a sad affair; she has at length become sensible
of the impropriety of her conduct, and now hopes to
atone for it by flattering every gentleman she sees —
time will show whether this plan will succeed. She
talks incessantly, laughs always at what she says herself. At table, when the judges, lawyers, and a dozen
gentlemen and ladies were seated, Miss P—— engrossed
all the conversation. I defy any person to be in the
room with her and not be compelled to converse with
her, not by the irresistible force of her charms, they
are rather in the wane. If you look at her she asks

what you were going to say — " I know you were going
to speak by your looks." Of course my gentleman
walks up, how can he help it ? In this manner she
draws a whole swarm around her ; the poor souls rattle
out their outrageous compliments, trembling with fear,
for the moment their ardor to please appears to abate,
she rouses them to a sense of their duty by a lash of
her tongue.

Sunday. — Now I can't bear to be hurried, and I must
submit to be or not send this by Mamma King. Last
night when I began this, I felt quite disposed to throw
away an hour (for my letters to you are thrown away as
you won't take the trouble to answer them) without consulting anything but my feelings. I began, and soon
found, to my mortification, that I ought to have consulted my candle, for as if piqued at my neglect, it took
French leave to doze. I broke off my description of
Miss P—— in the most *striking* part. I do not resume
the subject, 'twould be a profanation of this day to
scandalize a frail sister ; my mind is full of charity and
Christian love. I hope I shall not stumble against some
unlucky thought that may derange its present peaceful
state. Now, Cousin, don't you think it unpardonable,
don't you think it a violation of all the laws of politeness, that you should neglect writing me merely because I owed a letter? I should not be surprised if you
counted the words in yours and my letters and settled
the account by some rule in Arithmetic. But let me
entreat you not to estimate mine by the *weight*, but the

number ; in that case I am equal to anybody ; but if,
unhappily for me, you should weigh them with critical
exactness, 'twill take many of them to repay you for
one of yours. I feel assured you must have adopted
this method, and sincerely ask your pardon for doubting
a moment that this was the true cause. What prevented your coming to Wiscassett? I tho't you had
determined upon it. Rebecca and I used to expect you
every day ; believe me I was asked a dozen times if you
were not absolutely engaged to Miss Rice. How such
things will get about. I told every body that asked me
that I was your confidant, of course must keep your
attachment a secret, for which I am prepared to receive
your thanks.

Mr. Kinsman has been down to Wiscassett. He
attended the courts, as he says, to acquire a better
knowledge of the law ; but I should imagine he mis-
took the *ladies* for the *law*, as he makes them his constant study. But I leave so dangerous a subject, lest
my feelings should deprive me of the power to finish this sheet. I shall probably return home the beginning of next month. If I have a letter due from
you, according to your new arrangement, I beg you to
forward it as soon as possible ; however, I have not the
vanity to suppose there is more than a dozen lines as
yet ; perhaps when I have written half a dozen more
letters I may be *richly* rewarded with *one* from you.
Where is Maria? How does she do? Rebecca wrote
her while I was in Wiscassett, and told her undoubtedly

she is expected to spend the winter there.   I must finish: Uncle calls.   Eliza.

I believe it is about the 10th day of October.   E.

Ellen Coffin is going to be married to a widower and 3 children, think of that, sir!!!   I had a letter from her last week.   She is not coming home till she leaves Portland as Mrs. Derby.

Topsham, Oct. 29, 1801.

Why, you unaccountable wretch! you obstinate fellow! you malicious, you vain, you — Oh, I am run out, I will e'en call in the assistance of Sir John Fallstaff to help me exclaim against you — provoking creature! With one scratch of your pen to banish such delightful thoughts!   I was applauding myself for my *condescension* in writing so often without answers.   I exulted in the thought of your shame and confusion at the proofs of my superiority, — so much above the little forms that narrowed your own heart.   How did I see you hanging your head with penitence and sorrow, while your face glowed with conscious shame!   Oh, 'twas delicious!   Every day I reflected on it with renewed pleasure.   I felt assured nothing prevented your writing but an aversion to acknowledging how humble, how little you felt, — yet the letter at length arrived, my heart trembled with delight, a glow of triumph flushed my face.   I saw the humiliation so grateful to my vanity, (I was at the *Lieu* table) — I hurried the

letter into my pocket, I had no wish to read it — I knew
(I tho't I did) what it *must* contain. I could scarcely
breathe ; vanity, exultation, revenge (sweet sensation)
gave me unusual spirits. I stood and called 5 — I was
sure of a Palm-flush ! 'twas impossible anything could
go wrong, — 'twas a frail hope — I got nothing, was
lieued ; never mind it, thought I, the letter is enough. I
played wrong, discarded the wrong card, knocked over
the candlestick, spilt my wine ; positively, if it had been
a love-letter, a first declaration, it would not put me in
a worse flustration ; but ah ! 't was so different, — I did
not blush, look down, tremble, fear to raise my eyes ;
my heart did not dissolve away in melting tenderness —
hey-day ! I had no notion of telling you what I did *not*
do — but what I *did*. Well then — I sat so upright, I
was a foot taller, I looked at every body for applause. I
wondered I did not hear them exclaim : Oh, generous,
excellent girl ! I demanded it with my eyes — 'twas
all in vain, I heard nothing but — " Eliza, you must follow suit. Why do you play that card ? You will certainly be lieued ! " I was vexed ; I thought of the letter,
all was sunshine again. I am called — dinner ; oh, this
eating seems to clog all my faculties, I never write with
half so much ease as when I'm half starved. I believe
it is true that poets ought not to live well.

But begging your pardon for leaving you so in the
lurch, I had forgotten that the letter was as yet un-
opened in my pocket. Well then, we did not break up
till late ; after I retired to bed out came the letter. I

was sleepy and had a great mind not to open it till morning ; however I thought I would, to have the satisfaction of the confirmation of my hopes, not once thinking of the stroke that should annihilate them.   It came. How shall I tell you my consternation ! — "description falters at the threshold ; " yet I did not rave, I did not tear my hair with a frenzy of passion.   I did not stand in mute despair, — no ; I collected all my dignity and stood fixed and immovable.   I was convinced 'twas obstinacy alone, 'twas envy, 'twas a something that prevented you from giving me what you knew I deserved. I am called again.

Portland, Nov. 10, 1801.

I had almost determined to light the fire with this scrawl ! — but upon second thoughts I withdrew my hand from the devouring flames and saved it from the fate it so justly merits.   Yet we have such a partiality for our own offspring we rarely ever treat them with the severity they deserve.   But I ought to tell you where I am, — but this letter has nothing like method in it — but never mind — I began it immediately after I received your last.   I wrote while the first impressions it made were on me ; unluckily I was called from the pleasing task while in the midst of it, and as I never feel the same two hours together, I was unable to continue as I began : 'twould have been cold and studied ; so I left it.   I threw it into my trunk, determining not to have anything more to do with it.   I had grown amazingly wise; I wondered how I could suffer myself to write such nonsense. To-day I have received an invitation to the *second* wedding of Capt. Stephenson. I shall go. I thought I would write you a line to let you know I was still in existence and on my way home. I could not find any paper and was compelled to tumble over my trunk to find this. I have a world of news to tell you, but I don't know that you would care a farthing about any of it. Mary has been at Boston. Capt. Stephenson told me all about it. Tell her I hear she has a heap of fine things, at which, together with her ladyship, I hope to have a peep. I have something of vast importance to say to *her* likewise, a thing on which depends the life and happiness of a fellow-creature. "Oh, Mary! who would have thought cruelty one of the failings of your heart." But I shall out with this secret to you before I am aware of it. Now I have a great mind to turn this into a letter to Mary. I have as much again to say to her as I have to you, but she would not know what to make of some of it. I expect to be at home on Saturday next; bring Mary on Sunday, — mind, and don't disobey. Horatio will be with me. I am in a monstrous hurry. I must send more blank paper than I ever did before, for which you will thank me, as I think you once told me that the blank paper in my letters always afforded you the most pleasure, — not exactly so — but something like it. Adieu.

ELIZA.

Mr. Moses Porter.

Scarborough, Dec. 4th, 1801.

"I give you thanks," as Parson Fletcher says, for your dissertation upon apologies and old sayings. You have stored up enough to fill a volume, if I should take your last as a specimen of the quantity. However, they are things I trouble myself but little about, and I should rather be inclined to join in railing against them than in enumerating their good effects. I perceive that you were much more inclined to be their advocate after supper than you were before. You had just laid down your pen after venting all your spleen and ill-nature (occasioned by your impatience for roast-beef) upon these poor harmless old sayings. You return, with an entire new set of sentiments on the subject. You commence their advocate with more vehemence than is usual with you, and conclude by making them the very foundation of every virtue. Now I have endeavored to find some natural cause for this sudden change, but cannot. Was it that you heard one trickle from the lips of some favorite fair with eloquence too powerful to be resisted? Or was it a bumper of wine which proved so warm a friend to them? Or was it the good-natured effects of the roast-beef, which exhilarating your spirits, made you look with an eye of pity and compassion on these poor neglected things, and endeavor by rubbing off the rust and polishing them anew, to compensate for your malicious endeavors to lessen their merit? But after all I must confess my-

self a great enemy to them, in conversation particularly. I never knew a person who made frequent use
of them, but I pitied them for the scanty portion of
ideas which must have driven them to such a paltry
theft; and moreover, if I must steal the idea, I would
clothe it myself, lest its garment should betray me. I
dislike them because they are in every body's mouth,
the greatest fool on earth has sense enough to use
them with as much propriety as any other, and you will
find every old beggar has his wallet stuffed full of them,
ready to launch out on every occasion. I don't know,
however, but you are perfectly right in what you say in
their defence. I am inclined to believe what you say
is just, but I have so often seen instances of their
meaning being perverted to answer some vicious purpose that I am compelled to believe the balance is
against them. "So much for old sayings." — But now
as to apologies, I must with *due reverence* beg leave to
differ from you in my opinion of them. I am by no
means inclined to think they are never used but when
we know ourselves in fault, and that we ought always
to suspect the sincerity of any one who makes them.
You certainly must have known instances when they
were essentially necessary, and not to have made them
would have proved an obstinacy of disposition quite as
disagreeable as insincerity. I hate this parade and nonsense about *independence*, which every gentleman of *ton*
puts on ; it always proves that the reality is small, when
such a fuss is made for the appearance. I know some

gentlemen who boast of never having made an apology, yet at the same time would say and do a thousand things much more derogatory to their dear independence than fifty apologies, such as any man of sense might make.   I should be glad to see our fine gentlemen more careful in avoiding anything that would require an apology, and not like cowards skulk behind their flimsy shield of independence for defence or security.   I have as great an aversion to cringing apologies, made on every occasion, as you possibly can have, and should always suspect the sincerity of them. — If this class are the greater part of them, — still I can conceive, nay I *have known* instances when an apology has heightened my opinion of a person instead of lessening it.   If we are in fault, ought we not to confess it ?   If we are *not* in fault, ought we not to exculpate ourselves ?   I should think a person valued my approbation very little, if he knew I had any reason to censure him and yet would not by a single word convince me I had been deceived.   However, I did not mean to dip so far into this *weighty* subject, 'twould have been better to have just touched the edges and away.   Now really, Moses, I write in pain if I am not good-natured ; you must attribute it all to the cold which makes my fingers tingle ; I can't write below, there is such a gabbling.   'Tis a cold, comfortless night ; the rain patters against the window and the wind whistles round the house, it sounds like December, — oh ! that was an unlucky word !   I feel gloomy at the sight of it.   The

storm has driven all my thoughts back to myself for
shelter. I am at this moment so selfish and cross that
I would not walk ten steps to do good to any one. Our
old windows here clatter so that I can hear nothing
else. I shall begin to think the candle burns blue, and
that I hear the groans of distress between the blasts
of wind, which sound hollow and dreary ; even now the
shadow of my pen on the wall looked like a man's arm,
and as true as I live, here is a winding-sheet in the
candle. Oh these hobgoblin stories ! we never get rid
of them. I sometimes, when sitting alone, after all are
asleep in the house, get my imagination so roused, that
I look in fearful expectation that the tall martial ghost
of Hamlet will stalk before my eyes, or that some less
dignified one will step through the keyhole, or pop
down chimney. — Ghosts, what a looking word that is !!
— nonsense !— what was I going to say, something
about ghosts and all not warming my fingers. I declare
this shall be the last letter I will write from the fire, —
December, and writing in the chamber without fire.
Oh — monstrous ! But here am I at the end without
saying several things I meant to. I never, when I sit
down to write, say any thing I wished or intended to
when I began. You found my letter, you say — 'twas
not worth the finding, as it was too late to answer the
purpose I wish. Write me often. I have been enter-
tained with Johnson's life. We are alone, so write me
often.   E. S.

A man of your gallantry, cousin, surely might make a small exertion to confer an obligation on two of the fair. Octavia and myself are very anxious that Miss Tappan should make us a visit. My father will bring Miranda home; but our chaise is broken so much that 'tis impossible to use it in its present state; none to be hired or borrowed. Why can't you take a chaise and bring over Pauline and Betsey Tappan? Besides gratifying me with their company, I would be very glad to see you — no coaxing Eliza! But I am in earnest; come and see. Do come and bring them if possible. I will show you some of Martha's letters from London, Bath. I will tell you everything I can think of and perhaps invent something if all this won't do. Lord bless me! I should not have to urge every one so hard to come and see me. I am sure I should be discouraged; but seriously, I wish you to come *very* much, but if you think it *impossible*, or rather very bad — don't mind what I say; however, I expect you.   Eliza.

To Mr. Moses Porter.

Portland, Jan. 24, 1802.

Now at this moment imagine your friend Eliza half-double with the cold, two children teazing and playing round the table, sister and nurse talking all the time, and you will then be prepared to receive a letter abounding with sound reasoning, profound argument, elegant language, and a profusion of sublime ideas; but do not stare if I intersperse, by way of relieving your mind, a

few little Jackey Horner stories which I am obliged to
gabble out by wholesale to stop the children's mouths.
If I had not had a most retentive memory, I should have
forgotten we were correspondents. I can put up with
such a tardy, indifferent, reluctant correspondent when
I myself set the example — but we ladies are so accustomed to attention from gentlemen that I can hardly
bring myself to put up with your neglect. I have a
thousand times determined to wait just as long before I
answer your letters as you do before mine are noticed,
and you have nothing to prevent — but, pshaw! I am
only spending time to give you something to laugh at. I
must honestly acknowledge, however, that your last letter was very *acceptable*, though I was piqued at your neg-
lecting me so long. I wish I felt adequate to giving
an opinion on your perfect character, but as I have told
you before, I cannot *think* when all is noise and confusion around me. But I have endeavored in vain to find
fault with it. I am really sorry that your sentiments so
perfectly coincide with my own, for you have said all I
think on the subject and much more than I could have
expressed, therefore I am compelled to assent to all you
have said. I am very glad we do not agree on every
subject, for our letters would (mine I mean) be very un-
entertaining, indeed they have no merit to part with. I
do not mean to send your perfect character away without a more intimate acquaintance. When I feel in a
proper mood for it I will take it up and examine every
quality separately. I have the outlines impressed on

my mind, but I cannot refer to your letter for 'tis up in
my trunk and I feel no disposition to leave the fire ; with
your permission I will lay it by till another time.   In
the meantime let us descend from these important discussions to the trifling occurrences of the day.   With
great satisfaction we at length behold the ground covered with snow, for we are almost freezing here ; it has
been impossible almost to obtain wood to keep us warm,
and I declare I have thought a log-house and clay chimney —The bell rings — I must stop ! —

Monday, Feb. 1, 1802, Portland.

The sudden ringing of the bell last Monday stopt
me in the midst of a very homely catalogue of blessings
— 'tis not worth finishing, and if it was I could not take
up a broken sentence and finish it a week after it was
begun.   I have in vain attempted to finish this sheet,
but I find I am entirely unfit to write.   I hold my pen
firm in my hand, look this side and that side, yet still
cannot think.   Scarborough — desolate, dreary Scarborough is the only place from whence I can write with
ease, — nothing present engages my attentions, and I
then have leisure to turn over the rubbish which I have
collected from home — ponder on things past and anticipate those to come : 'tis something like dreaming, — we
are insensible to everything around us, — the imagination is unchecked by the operation of our senses, and

soars beyond the boundaries of reality. Pray read over this last half-page and see if you cannot tell how I feel, look, and act at this moment. If your penetration does not discover a something unlike my letters in general, — cold and studied — I will not — I cannot write, another post must pass and no letter, yet 'tis labor, 'tis pain to write thus.

Sunday, Feb. 8.

To see the dates of this sheet one would immediately conclude that my ideas flowed periodically and that I had stated periods to "unpack the heart," but 'tis because I cannot take my pen and write at the moment I feel an inclination, — not to defer it till a more convenient time when I most probably should feel indifferent about it. Now I am aware what you are about to infer from such a dull studied letter as this is, — The "seven days twice run" has put something into your head that ought not to be there, and you are laughing in your sleeve at the discovery. Now, I am not after the manner of our sex going to protest it is false — that there is no foundation for such a report, and counterfeit anger that I don't feel, for these things always are viewed as a modest confirmation of the truth, and frequently are considered the greatest proof that can be brought. It is folly to give importance to such stories by appearing to feel interested, and the only way to destroy them is to hear and let them pass with perfect indifference ; time will certainly show what is true and what is not, and the only method is to let them take their course, they will sink to oblivion if not fed by our own folly. I own 'tis unpleasant to hear such things, but every girl must prepare herself for such vexations. It has one good effect — that of making us more circumspect in our conduct. I do not say I am not in love; if your penetration has not discovered that I *am*, neither will what I say convince you. How such a report came to you I do not know. I had hoped it would wither and die in the hotbed of scandal from whence it sprang. If you lived here you would not be surprised at any thing of the kind. I declare to you I don't know the girl in town of whom the same is not said. The prevailing propensity this winter is *match-making*, and at the assemblies there is no other conversation, — such and such a one will make a match because they dance together, — another one is positively engaged because she does *not* dance with him. If a lady does not attend the assembly constantly — 'tis because her favorite swain is not a member, — if she does — 'tis to meet him there : if she is silent, she is certainly in love ; if she is gay and talks much, there must be a lover in the way. If a gentleman looks at you at meeting you are suspected, if he dances with you at the assembly it must be true, and if he *rides* with you — 'tis " confirmation strong as proof of holy writ." I am vext to have spent so much time on this subject, but I care nothing about it. 'Tis well I have found something to fill my sheet, and had it not been for that lucky seven days twice over, I should not have finished it this month, and finishing now has been a *week's* work. ELIZA.

To Mr. Moses Porter.

Sunday, Feb'y 14.

Only think, Moses, I was from home when you passed thro' town! I did not expect you so soon, altho' you said you should return on Friday. I thought *something* might detain you in Wiscassett longer than you expected; but you are one of those odd fellows which nothing can turn aside, no, not even the most sparkling pair of black eyes in the world could detain you a moment longer than you first intended, — what a philosopher in this age of gallantry to remain untainted! It will come at last, Moses. Belamy says there is as much a time for love as for death, and every one as surely one time or other will feel it. I expect to see you throw off the Philosopher and assume the man ; one more trial and I will pronounce you invulnerable. For Miss T——, this one is reserved. I long to see how you will look when (to use a religious phrase) you are struck down. Pray write me as soon as you receive this and tell me about your journey ; don't wait as long as you commonly do.

Adieu. ELIZA.

Portland, March 1, 1802.

Such a frolic! Such a chain of adventures I never before met with, nay, the page of romance never presented its equal. 'Tis now Monday, — but a little more method, that I may be understood. I have just ended my Assembly's adventure, never got home till this morning. Thursday it snowed violently, indeed for two days before it had been storming so much that the snow drifts were very large; however, as it was the last Assembly I could not resist the temptation of going, as I knew all the world would be there. About 7 I went down-stairs and found young Charles Coffin, the minister, in the parlor. After the usual enquiries were over he stared awhile at my feathers and flowers, asked if I was going out, — I told him I was going to the Assembly. "Think, Miss Southgate," said he, after a long pause, "think you would go out to *meeting* in such a storm as this?" Then assuming a tone of reproof, he entreated me to examine well my feelings on such an occasion. I heard in silence, unwilling to begin an argument that I was unable to support. The stopping of the carriage roused me; I immediately slipt on my. socks and coat, and met Horatio and Mr. Motley in the entry. The snow was deep, but Mr. Motley took me up in his arms and sat me in the carriage without difficulty. I found a full assembly, many married ladies, and every one disposed to end the winter in good spirits. At one we left dancing and went to the card-room to wait for a coach. It stormed dreadfully. The hacks were all employed as soon as they returned, and we could not get one till 3 o'clock, for about two they left the house, determined not to return again for the night. It was the most violent storm I ever knew. There were now 20 in waiting, the gentlemen scolding and fretting, the ladies murmuring and complaining. One hack returned; all flocked to the stairs to engage a seat. So many crowded down that 'twas impossible to get past; luckily I was one of the first. I stept in, found a young lady, almost a stranger in town, who keeps at Mrs. Jordan's, sitting in the back-seat. She immediately caught hold of me and beg'd if I possibly could accommodate her to take her home with me, as she had attempted to go to Mrs. Jordan's, but the drifts were so high, the horses could not get through; that they were compelled to return to the hall, where she had not a single acquaintance with whom she could go home. I was distres't, for I could not ask her home with me, for sister had so much company that I was obliged to go home with Sally Weeks and give my chamber to Parson Coffin. I told her this, and likewise that she should be provided for if my endeavors could be of any service. None but ladies were permitted to get into the carriage; it presently was stowed in so full that the horses could not move; the door was burst open, for such a clamor as the closing of it occasioned I never before heard. The universal cry was — "a gentleman in the coach, let him come out!" We all

protested there was none, as it was too dark to distinguish ; but the little man soon raised his voice and bid
the coachman proceed ; a dozen voices gave contrary
orders. 'Twas a proper riot, I was really alarmed. My
gentleman, with a vast deal of fashionable independence,
swore no power on earth should make him quit his seat ;
but a gentleman at the door jump't into the carriage,
caught hold of him, and would have dragged him out if
we had not all entreated them to desist. He squeezed
again into his seat, inwardly exulting to think he
should get safe home from such rough creatures as the
men, should pass for a lady, be secure under their protection, for none would insult him before them, mean
creature !! The carriage at length started full of ladies,
and not one gentleman to protect us, except our lady
man who had crept to us for shelter. When we found
ourselves in the street, the first thing was to find out
who was in the carriage and where we were all going,
who first must be left. Luckily two gentlemen had
followed by the side of the carriage, and when it stopt
took out the ladies as they got to their houses. Our
sweet little, trembling, delicate, unprotected fellow sat
immovable whilst the two gentlemen that were obliged
to walk thro' all the snow and storm carried all the
ladies from the carriage. What could be the motive of
the little wretch for creeping in with us I know not : I
should have thought 'twas his great wish to serve the
ladies, if he had moved from the seat, but 'twas the
most singular thing I ever heard of. We at length

arrived at the place of our destination. Miss Weeks
asked Miss Coffin (for that was the unlucky girl's name)
to go home with her, which she readily did. The gentlemen then proceeded to take us out. My beau, unused
to carrying such a weight of sin and folly, sank under
its pressure, and I was obliged to carry my mighty self
through the snow which almost buried me. Such a
time, I never.shall forget it! My great-grandmother
never told any of her youthful adventures to equal it.
The storm continued till Monday, and I was obliged to
stay ; but Monday I insisted if there was any possibility
of getting to Sister's to set out. The horse and sleigh
were soon at the door, and again I sallied forth to brave
the tempestuous weather (for it still snowed) and surmount the many obstacles I had to meet with. We
rode on a few rods, when coming directly upon a large
drift, we stuck fast. We could neither get forward nor
turn round. After waiting till I was most frozen we got
out, and with the help of a truckman the sleigh was
lifted up and turned towards a cross street that led to
Federal Street. We again went on ; at the corner we
found it impossible to turn up or turn, but must go
down and begin where we first started, and take a new
course ; but suddenly turning the corner we came full
upon a pair of trucks, heavily laden ; the drift on one
side was so large that it left a very narrow passage
between that and the corner house, indeed we were
obliged to go so near that the post grazed my bonnet.
What was to be done? Our horses' heads touched

before we saw them. I jump't out, the sleigh was un-
fastened and lifted round, and we again measured back
our old steps. At length we arrived at Sister Boyd's
door, and the drift before it was the greatest we had
met with; the horse was so exhausted that he sunk
down, and we really thought him dead. 'Twas some
distance from the gate and no path. The gentleman
took me up in his arms and carried me till my weight
pressed him so far into the snow that he had no power
to move his feet. I rolled out of his arms and wal-
lowed till I reached the gate; then rising to shake off
the snow, I turned and beheld my beau fixed and im-
moveable; he could not get his feet out to take another
step. At length, making a great exertion to spring his
whole length forward, he made out to reach the poor
horse, who lay in a worse condition than his master.
By this time all the family had gathered to the window,
indeed they saw the whole frolic; but 'twas not yet
ended, for, unluckily, in pulling off Miss Weeks' bonnet
to send to the sleigh to be carried back, I pulled off my
wig and left my head bare. I was perfectly convulsed
with laughter. Think what a ludicrous figure I must
have been, still standing at the gate, my bonnet half-
way to the sleigh and my wig in my hand. However, I
hurried it on, for they were all laughing at the window,
and made the best of my way into the house. The horse
was unhitched and again set out, and left me to ponder
on the incidents of the morning. I have since heard of
several events that took place that Assembly night

much more amusing than mine, — nay, Don Quixote's most ludicrous adventures compared with some of them will appear like the common events of the day.

March 12, 1802.

William Weeks is going to Philipsburg[1] and thinks of returning by the way of Scarborough; if so, will leave this at our house, otherwise can return it to me. I have not yet seen Miss Jewett, but I hear she has returned. Did your Saco party come as you expected? Give my love to Miss Tappan, and tell her nothing but the fame of her beauty would carry this young man so many miles out of his way. I found he was very desirous of calling at our house, therefore wrote by him. Tell her she must answer for the mischief done by leading young men astray from their path. I will estimate the loss it will be to William : — he will ride 6 or 8 miles further than necessary, — fatigue his horse, — wear out his sleigh runners, and certainly be detained 3 hours. Now, as we know a gentleman's time is much more valuable than a lady's, it must be a real loss to him. 3 dollars a day for posting books any common accountant would have; and allowing him but just so much, his loss would certainly amount to 4 — 6 on that score. I speak merely of the loss on the score of interest; — how deeply it may affect him otherwise may better be imagined from the ravages she has committed in Mr. Orr's heart than from any thing I can say. This short visit may derange all his

[1] Phippsburg.

reasoning faculties, and give a different hue to all his
future prospects, — it may give him a disrelish for all
amusements, and make him sigh for the calm serenity
of domestic life, — to sum up all together — it may
make him *in love*, — but I shall have no time to say
anything else, if I run on with this any further. To-
morrow I expect to go to Gorham, — return the same
evening or Sunday morning. I am still at Mrs. Coffin's,
but shall return to Sister when I come from Gorham.
We have had a number of pleasant parties this week, —
Tuesday Mrs. Robert Boyd had a charming one.
Wednesday had a large one here, and to-day all going to
Capt. Robinson's, where we expect to dance. To-morrow I go to Gorham. I wrote to Mamma requesting
money to buy a lace shade, — I called to look at them
again and the shopkeeper told me he was mistaken in
the price, for it was 21 per yard instead of the whole
pattern, which makes a vast difference. I, of course,
think no more of lace shades, but I still think of some
money, I have but 4 cents in the world, not enough to
pay the postage of a letter, pray send me a little immediately. I shall send you a description of the Assembly
— which I believe you may read to my Mother if you
wish, 'twill amuse her I know. I wish you would look
in the old desk among my papers and get a little Drawing book, — directions for drawing printed in a pam-
phlet, and give to William to bring over. I hope the
snow will last till Mamma comes over and I return
home, 'tis delightful weather. How do the daisies and

jelly flowers ? Mrs. Parker is going to give me some
flower seeds. I hear frequent enquiries for you — when
are you coming in town ? Tell Miss Tappan I had the
honor of dancing a voluntary dance with Mr. Orr at the
last assembly, — he attracted much attention by his irregular expression — " The floor was very *unyielding*,"
&c., &c. I did not tell you any one's adventures but
my own on that eventful night. Poor Mr. Orr, impatient to get home, plunged into the snow without waiting for a carriage, and unfortunately turning up street
instead of down, got most to Mr. Vaughn's before he
discovered his mistake, and was obliged to turn round
and worry his way back again, he was half dead when
he got to his lodgings. Eunice Deering was tumbled
over and when Mr. Little took her from the carriage[1] .

.   .   .   .

Portland, May 23, 1802.

I receive your apology and am satisfied — 'tis not the
manner of making apologies I think most of, but that
long dissertation on the subject continually obtrudes itself on your mind whenever you feel conscious an apology is necessary, but while I am convinced nothing but
the fear of appearing inconsistent prevents your making
these said apologies, I will not complain — let them
come " edgeways " or any other way — so long as I am
convinced you feel their necessity. But I have been
pondering on your new plan of life, yet I confess it does

[1] This letter was never finished.

not appear to me so delightful as to you, it sounds well,
— tickles the fancy, — cuts a pretty figure on paper
and would form a delightful chapter for a novel.   Our
novelists have worn the pleasures of rural life threadbare, every lovesick swain imagines that with the mistress of his heart he could leave the noisy tumultuous
scenes of life and in the shades of rural retirement feel
all the delightful serenity and peace ascribed to the
golden age.   The Philosopher and the Poet fly to this
imaginary heaven with as much enthusiasm as the lover.
Here, say they, we can contemplate the beauty and sublimity of nature free from interruption ; here the reflecting mind can find endless subjects for contemplation !
here all is peace and love ! no discord can find a place
among these innocent and happy beings, — they live
but to promote the happiness of each other and their
every action teems with benevolence and love.   Yet let
us judge for ourselves, — we all have seen what the
pleasures of rural life are, and whatever Poets may have
ascribed to it, we must know there is as much depravity
and consequently as much discontent in the inhabitants
of a country village as in the most populous city.   They
are generally ignorant, illiterate, without knowledge to
discover the real blessings they enjoy by comparing
them with others, continually looking to those above
them with envy and discontent and imagine their share
of happiness is proportioned to their rank and power.
I am convinced that a country life is more calculated
to produce that security and happiness we are all in
pursuit of than any other, but those who have ever been

accustomed to it have no relish for its pleasures, and those who quit the busy scenes of life, disgusted by the duplicity or ingratitude of the world, or oppressed by the weight of accumulated misfortune — carry with them feelings and sentiments which cannot be reciprocated. Solitary happiness I have no idea of, 'tis only in the delightful sympathies of friendship, similarity of sentiments, that genuine happiness can be enjoyed. Your mind is cultivated and enlarged, your sentiments delicate and refined, you could not expect to find many with whom you could converse on a perfect equality, — or rather many whose sentiments could assimilate with yours. Were I a man, I should think it cowardly to bury myself in solitude, — nay, I should be unwilling to confess I felt myself unable to preserve my virtue where there were temptations to destroy it, there is no merit in being virtuous when there is no struggle to preserve that virtue. 'Tis in the midst of temptations and allurements that the active and generous virtues must be exerted in their full force. One virtuous action where there were temptations and delusions to surmount would give more delight to my own heart, more real satisfaction than a whole life spent in more negative goodness, he must be base indeed who can voluntarily act wrong when no allurement draws him from the path of virtue. You say you never dip't much into the pleasures of *high life* and therefore should have but little to regret on that score. In the choice of life one ought to consult their own dispositions and inclinations, their own powers and talents. We all have a preference to some particular mode of life, and we surely ought to endeavor to arrive at that which will more probably ensure us most happiness.   I have often thought what profession I should choose were I a man.   I might then think very differently from what I do now, yet I have always thought if I felt conscious of possessing brilliant talents, the *law* would be my choice.   Then I might hope to arrive at an eminence which would be gratifying to my feelings.   I should then hope to be a public character, respected and admired, — but unless I was convinced I possessed the talents which would distinguish me as a speaker I would be anything rather than a lawyer ; — from the dry sameness of such employments as the business of an office all my feelings would revolt, but to be an eloquent speaker would be the delight of my heart. I thank Heaven I was *born* a woman.   I have now only patiently to wait till some clever fellow shall take a fancy to me and place me in a situation, I am determined to make the best of it, let it be what it will.   We ladies, you know, possess that "sweet pliability of temper" that disposes us to enjoy any situation, and we must have no choice in these things till we find what is to be our destiny, then we must consider it the best in the world.   But remember, I desire to be thankful I am not a man.   I should not be content with moderate abilities — nay, I should not be content with mediocrity in any thing, but as a woman I am equal to the generality of my sex, and I do not feel that great desire of fame I think I should if I was a man.   Should you hereafter become an inhabitant of Boyford I make no doubt you will be very happy, because you will weigh all the advantages and disadvantages. Yet I do not think you qualified for the laborious life farmers generally lead, and it requires a little fortune to live an independent farmer without labor. Rebecca would do charmingly, I know you are imagining her the partner of all your joys and cares, — of all your harmony and content, when you charm yourself with your description of rural happiness. With her you imagined you could quit the world and almost live happy in a desert. So may it be, — I know none but a lover could paint the sweets of retirement with such enthusiasm. 'Tis *my* turn now to rail a little, — the world also has linked *you* to a certain person, as firmly — nay, *more* so than it ever did me; however I will not press so closely on this subject. I shall not expect that candid confession I made you, — as your feelings and mine are, I believe, entirely different on the two subjects. I want to ask you a question which you may possibly think improper, but if so, do not answer it. — Is Mary [1] really engaged to Mr. Coffin? I hear so from so many persons and in so decided a manner I cannot doubt. I would ask her, but in these things there is so much deception, there is no finding out, — but however, I think I should never deny such a thing when I once was engaged, — however, enough of this. I am now in Portland, shall return to-morrow to Scarborough where I shall be very happy to see you and Mary, so I depend on your bringing her over very soon.

[1] Mary King Porter (at this time twenty years of age) married Nathan Coffin.

Adieu— dinner is ready and I have nothing to say worth losing it for, write me often — I shall be at home alone these two months to come, — remember you have it in your power to amuse and gratify.　　　Eliza.

I hardly know what to say to you, Cousin, you have attacked my system with a kind of fury that has entirely obscured your judgment, and instead of being convinced of its impracticability, you appear to fear its justness. You tell me of some excellent effects of my system, but pardon me for thinking they are dictated by prejudice rather than reason. I feel fully convinced in my own mind that no such effects could be produced. You ask if this plan of education will render one a more dutiful child, a more affectionate wife, &c, &c., surely it will, — those virtues which now are merely practised from the momentary impulse of the heart, will then be adhered to from principle, a sense of duty, and a mind sufficiently strengthened not to yield implicitly to every impulse, will give a degree of uniformity, of stability to the female character, which it evidently at present does not possess. From having no fixed guide for our conduct we have acquired a reputation for caprice, which we justly deserve. I can hardly believe you serious when you say that "the enlargement of the mind will inevitably produce superciliousness and a desire of ascendancy," — I should much sooner expect it from an ignorant, uncultivated mind. We cannot enlarge and improve our minds without perceiving our weakness, and wisdom is always modest and unassuming, — on the contrary a mind that has never been exerted knows not its deficiencies and presumes much more on its powers than it otherwise would. You beg me to drop this crazy scheme and say no more about enlarging the mind, as it is disagreeable, and you are too much prejudiced ever to listen with composure to me when I write on the subject. I quit it forever, nor will I again shock your ear with a plan which you think has nothing for its foundation either just or durable, which a girlish imagination gave birth to, and a presumptuous folly cherished. I fear I have rather injured the cause than otherwise, and what I have said may have more firmly established those sentiments in you which I wished to destroy. Be it as it may, I believe it is a cause that has been more injured by its friends than its enemies. I am sorry that I have said so much, yet I said no more than I really thought, and still think, just and true. I beg you to say no more to me on the subject as I shall know 'twill be only a form of politeness which I will dispense with. You undoubtedly think I am acting out of my sphere in attempting to discuss this subject, and my presumption probably gave rise to that idea, which you expressed in your last, that however unqualified a woman might be she was always equipt for the discussion of any subject and overwhelmed her hearers with her "clack." On what subjects shall I write you ? I shall either fatigue and disgust you with female trifles, or shock you by stepping beyond the limits you have prescribed. As I cannot pursue a medium I fear I shall be obliged to relinquish the hope of pleasing — of course of writing.   Good night, I am sleepy and stupid. Morning.   O, how I hate this warm weather, it deprives me of the power of using any exertion, it clogs my ideas, and I ask no greater felicity than the pleasure of doing nothing.   I intended to amuse you with some of the trifles of the day, but I shall scarcely do them justice this morning.   Friday night we had a ball, — the hall was decorated with much taste.   'Twas filled up for the *masons.*   At the head of the room there was a most romantic little bower, four large pillars formed of green and interspersed with flowers, supported a kind of canopy which was arched in front, with this inscription — " Here Peace and Silence reign," filled with a parcel of girls whining sentiment, and silly fellows spouting love, it produced a most laughable scene.   The deities to whom it was dedicated withdrew from the sacred retreat, which was so profaned, and noise and folly reigned supreme, — so sweet a place, — so fine an opportunity for making speeches — 'twas irresistible, even *you* would have caught a spark of inspiration from the surrounding glories, — and felt a degree of emulation at the flashes of genius that blazed from every quarter. Invention was on the rack, the stores of memory were exhausted and folly blushed to be so outdone.   Mr. Symmes sat down to overwhelm me with a torrent of eloquence, yet his compassionate heart often prompted him to hesitate that I might recover myself.   Such stores of learning did he display, such mines of wisdom did he open to my view, that I gazed with astonishment

and awe and scarce believed " That one small head
could carry all he knew." Mr. Kinsman with a counte-
nance that beamed with benevolence and compassion
gazed on all around, while a benign smile played round
his mouth and dimpled his polished cheek, the laughing
loves peeped from his eyes and aimed their never-failing
darts — rash girl — too, too near hast thou approached
this divinity — the poisoned dart still rankles in thy
heart, — " The lingering pang of hopeless love unpitied
I endure," and feel a wound within my heart which
death alone can cure. Monday night — You will easily
perceive that I am obliged to write when and where I
can, I have not quite so much leisure as when at Scarborough, and though in the very place to *hear news*, I
have no faculty of relating what I hear in a manner that
could interest you. Last evening I spent in talking
scandal (for which God forgive me) but was too tempt-
ing an occasion to be resisted. I wish you were acquainted with some of the Portland ladies, I would then
tell you many things that might amuse. But I dare not
introduce you to them, lest I should entirely mistake
their character, and that when personally acquainted
with them you would be confirmed in your opinion of
my wanting penetration in studying characters. Yesterday I spent with Martha, I wish you were acquainted
with her, she is truly an *original.* I never saw one that
bore any resemblance to her. She despises flattery and
is even above praise, beautiful without vanity, possessing a refined understanding without pedantry, the most
exquisite sensibility connected with all the great and

noble qualities of the mind.   She knows that no woman in America ever was more admired, she has received every attention which could be paid and yet is exactly as before she left Portland.   The same condescension, the same elegance and unaffected simplicity of manners, the same independent and noble sentiments.   Perhaps I am blinded to her faults, yet I think she deserves all I say of her, nay more, for she "outstrips all praise and makes it halt behind her."   They have determined to go to England, in two months at farthest they will leave America, not to return for 2 years, — two years! how many, many events will have taken place.   Perhaps ere that I shall rest in the tomb of my fathers forgotten and unknown !!   Perhaps oppressed with care and borne down with misfortune, I shall have lost all relish for life —all hopes of pleasure may have ceased to exist and the grave of time closed over them forever.   I grow gloomy, I wish I could write anything, but I have never felt a relish for writing since I have been in Portland, — at home it supplies the place of *society*, but here I need no such substitute.   ELIZA.

Write by the post if you have no other opportunity, the players will commence acting next Wednesday.

I believe it is the 28th.

Mr. Moses Porter, Biddeford.

This letter is the last one written by Miss Southgate to her cousin Moses Porter.   The following one from Dr. Southgate to his brother-in-law, Rufus King, who

was then living in England, tells of the untimely death
of his nephew, and its sad cause, July 26th, 1802.

Our brother and sister Porter of Biddeford have
lost their eldest son Moses. He dyed (sic) about
fifteen days since of the yellow fever. He had a ship
arrived from the West Indies. On her passage the
cook boy dyed suddenly — the rest of the crew were
none of them sick, but of those persons who went on
board, five or six were taken with the yellow fever in
about four days — none of whom lived more than four
or five days. Moses is much lamented by his family
and acquaintance — this month would have completed
his law education. His talents, generous and amiable
disposition formed a pleasing prospect etc. etc. Mrs.
Porter's health is *better*, better than I ever expected
she would have enjoyed tho' she is now only a feeble
woman. R. SOUTHGATE.

JOURNAL.

Tuesday, July 6th, 1802.

Arrived in Salem, met Mrs. Derby at the door who
received us joyfully. At tea-time saw the children, fine
boys, very fond of Ellen and are managed by their
Father with great judgment. How few understand the
true art of managing children, and how often is the important task of forming young minds left to the discretion of servants who caress or reprove as the impulse
of the moment compels them. Here are we convinced
of the great necessity that Mothers, or all ladies should

have cultivated minds, as the first rudiments of education are always received from them, and at that early period of life when the mind is open to every new impression and ready to receive the seeds which must form the future principles of the character. At that time how important is it to be judicious in your conduct towards them! In the evening Mr. Hasket Derby came in on his return from New York; he is a fine, majestic-looking man, tho' he strikes you rather heavy and unwieldy on his first appearance; he says little, yet does not appear absent, — has travelled much, and in his manners has an easy unassuming politeness that is not the acquirement of a day. — Wednesday morning had an agreeable tete-a-tete with Ellen, talked over all our affairs: in the afternoon rode out to Hersey Derby's [1] farm, about 3 miles from Salem; a most delightful place! The gardens superior to any I have ever seen of the kind; cherries in perfection! We really feasted! There are 3 divisions in the gardens, and you pass from the lower one to the upper thro' several

[1] E. Hasket Derby, Jr., was born in Salem in 1766, and died in Londonderry, H. N., in 1826. Mr. Derby married, in 1797, Miss Lucy Brown. He was the son of E. Hasket Derby, who married Elizabeth Crowninshield, a leading merchant of Salem, and founder of the East India trade; known in the annals of Salem as "King Derby." Mr. Derby, the father, had four sons, who married and had families. They were E. Hasket, Jr., just mentioned; John, who married Miss Barton and secondly Miss Eleanor Coffin; E. Hersey, who married Miss Hannah Brown Fitch; and Richard C., who married Miss Martha Coffin. The father of E. Hasket Derby, Sen., was Richard Derby, merchant, a delegate to the Provincial Congress in 1774-5.

MR. E. HASKET DERBY of Salem. ÆT. 28.   1794.

From a miniature in possession of Dr. Hasket Derby of Boston.

arches rising one above the other. From the lower gate you have a fine perspective view of the whole range, rising gradually until the sight is terminated by a hermitage. The summer house in the center has an arch thro' it with 3 doors on each side which open into little apartments, and one of them opens to a staircase by which you ascend into a square room the whole size of the building; it has a fine airy appearance and commands a view of the whole garden ; two large chestnut trees on each side almost shade it from the view when seen from the sides; the air from the windows is always pure and cool, and the eye wanders with delight and admiration over the extensive landscape below, so beautifully variegated with the charms of nature. Imagination luxuriates with delight, and as it plays o'er the beauties of an opening flower, imperceptibly wanders to the first principles of nature, its wonderful and surprising operation ; its harmony and beauty. The room is ornamented with some Chinese figures and seems calculated for serenity and peace. 'Tis like the pavilion of Caroline, and I almost looked around me for the music of the Guitar and books ; but I heard not the tramplings of Lindorf's horse, nor did I sing to hear the echo of his voice, — "Listen to love, and thou shalt know indifference or bless the foe ; " certain it is, however, I thought of Caroline the moment I entered. We descended, and passing thro' the arch, proceeded to the hermitage, which terminated the garden. It was scarcely perceptible at a distance. A

large weeping-willow swept the roof with its branches
and bespoke the melancholy inhabitant. We caught a
view of the little hut as we advanced thro' the opening of the trees ; it was covered with bark, — a small
low door, slightly latched, immediately opened at our
touch. A venerable old man was seated in the centre
with a prayer-book in one hand, while the other supported his cheek, and rested on an old table, which,
like the hermit, seemed moulding to decay ; a broken
pitcher, a plate and tea-pot sat before him, and his tea-
kettle sat by the chimney ; a tattered coverlit was
spread over a bed of straw, which tho' hard might be
softened by resignation and content. I left him impressed with veneration and fear which the mystery of
his situation seemed to create. We returned to the
house, which was neat and handsome, and from thence
visited the Greenhouse, where we saw oranges and
lemons in perfection, — in one orange tree there were
green ones, ripe ones and blossoms. Every plant and
shrub which was beautiful and rare was collected here,
and I looked around with astonishment and delight ; at
the upper end of the garden there was a beautiful
arbour formed of a mound of turf, which we ascended
by several steps formed likewise of turf, and 'twas surrounded by a thick row of poplar trees which branched
out quite to the bottom and so close together that you
could not see through, — 'twas a most charming place,
and I know not how long we should have remained to
admire if they had not summoned us to tea. We re-

turned home, and Mr. Hasket Derby asked if we should
not like to walk over to his house and see the garden,
— we readily consented, as I had heard much of the
house. The evening was calm and delightful, the moon
shone in its greatest splendor. We entered the house,
and the door opened into a spacious entry ; on each side
were large white marble images. We passed on by doors
on each side opening into the drawing-room, dining-
room, parlor, etc., etc., and at the farther part of the
entry a door opened into a large, magnificent oval room ;
and another door opposite the one we entered was
thrown open and gave us a full view of the garden below. The moon shone with uncommon splendor. The
large marble *vases*, the images, the mirrors to corre-
spond with the windows, gave it so uniform and finished
an appearance, that I could not think it possible I
viewed objects that were real, every thing appeared like
enchantment, — the stillness of the hour, the imperfect
light of the moon, the novelty of the scene, filled my
mind with sensations I never felt before. I could not
realize every thing and expected every moment that the
wand of the fairy would sweep all from before my eyes
and leave me to stare and wonder what it meant. You
can scarcely conceive any thing more superb. We
descended into the garden, which is laid out with exquisite taste, an airy irregularity seems to characterize
the whole. At the foot of the garden there was a summer house, and a row of tall poplar trees which hid
every thing beyond from the sight, and formed a kind

of walk. I arrived there and to my astonishment found thro' the opening of the trees that there was a beautiful terrace the whole width of the garden; 'twas twenty feet from the street, and gravelled on the top, with a white balustrade round; 'twas almost level, and the poplar trees so close that we could only occasionally catch a glimpse of the house. The moon shone full upon it, and I really think this side is the most beautiful, tho' 'tis the back one. A large dome swells quite to the chamber-windows and is railed round on top and forms a delightful walk, — the magnificent pillars which support it fill the mind with pleasure. We returned into the house; and on passing the mirrors I involuntarily started back at seeing so much company in the other room. We entered the drawing-room which is superb, furnished with blue and wood color. There was the Grand Piano, the most charming Instrument I ever heard. Mr. and Mrs. Derby, Mr. Hasket D., Frank Coffin and myself were the party, and I was requested to play, and took my seat at the Instrument, and had just begun playing, when a slight noise in the entry made me turn my head. A gentleman entered and was introduced as Mr. Grey; made a most graceful bow, took his seat, and I resumed my playing. We rose to depart, and Mr. G. accompanied us home. I was delighted with his conversation, which was sensible, unassuming, and agreeable. I scarcely saw his face, as there was no light.

Thursday at home all day. In the evening walked

in the garden. The evening was uncommonly fine.
The moon shines brighter in Salem than anywhere
else ; here too is an elegant garden, full of fruit trees,
the walks kept as nice as possible, and shaded on
each side by plum trees ; very handsome summer house
where we sat an hour or two. Rambled in the garden all
the evening, which was the finest I ever saw, so very
light, that, as Shakespeare says, "'twas but the daylight
sick, only a little paler." There is something in a fine
moonlight evening exquisitely soothing to the soul. I
have felt as if I could melt away with the exquisite enthusiasm of my sensations. We were called into the
house and found Mrs. West, a sister of Mrs. Derby's ; but
more of her by-and-bye. Friday Dr. Coffin arrived, and
Dr. Lathrop and Hasket Derby dined with us and set
out for Boston.

The following letter, written by Martha Coffin, Eliza's
most intimate friend, and descriptive of a visit that she
paid to Salem, will be found of interest.

June 29, 1800.

My dear Ellen :

I have never told you all about my visit to Salem.
I passed my time as you may imagine very charmingly,
and had I your pen or your talent at description I
would endeavor to give you some ideas of the house,
the gardens, and the farm ; but it is *Impossible.*

The Hermitage more than answered my expectations. It is everything which we see described in novels, and which I thought was not to be found in reality.

The garden beyond description beautiful, does indeed exceed anything of the kind I ever saw. Ten thousand different kinds of flowers from all quarters of the globe. Fruit of every kind in abundance. A delightful Summer house in the middle of the garden, furnished quite in the rural style; and from the chamber where they sometimes drink tea is the most beautiful prospect you can imagine. M. COFFIN.

Salem, July 14, 1802.
Dear Mother:

I have just received my trunk with the letter and key. I perceive you have not received my letter by Mr. Jewett. Fear not, my dear Mother, tho' gay and volatile in my disposition, I feel that I shall return home with the same sentiments with which I left it. True, I was in the midst of gaiety and splendor such as I never before witnessed, yet a something within whispers true happiness resides not here, — in this family all is calm contentment and peaceful pleasure. Mr. Derby is everything his best friends can wish him, and the whole family consider him as every thing good and benevolent; he truly is so, and appears one of the finest men I ever knew. How is Uncle Porter's family? I

MRS. RICHARD DERBY. (MARTHA COFFIN.)

Miniature by Malbone, in possession of Miss Peabody of Boston.

cannot even now reconcile myself to the idea of leaving them so unexpectedly and so immediately, yet I know not how it could be avoided. I am in the midst of amusements and pleasure, they drive all melancholy reflection from my mind, but when alone, my feelings warmly pay a tribute to the merit of *our departed Moses*; yet I cannot, — do not realize, every thing contributes to make me think it a delusion, a mere dream; how is it possible I can realize it? Yet sometimes I feel it is, it must be true. How soon do we reconcile ourselves to the loss of the dearest friends; what would most distract us in anticipation we meet with calmness when it approaches; strange, unaccountable. I surely loved Moses with sincerity. I knew of no person so distantly connected whom I felt so interested in, — yet he is dead, — he is gone, and I can speak of it without emotion, and I am called. Adieu, I will write soon.

ELIZA.

JOURNAL.

Saturday, July 11, 1802.

We rode out, Ellen and myself, with the three boys, in a hack. Went to Danners — Parson Wadsworth's, to see Mrs. Rickman's children; took them in to ride; came down by the mills and went across to Hasket Derby's farm, — all the cherries gone, — rambled about the gardens an hour and returned home, — charming ride; the country round Salem is delightful, altho' 'tis situated rather in a plain, 'tis surrounded with beautiful hills, handsome trees, ponds, brooks, etc.   We got home at dusk and found Mr. Coffin just returned from Boston.   Mrs. Hasket Derby sent a great basket of cherries and her compliments, she would come over in the morning.   I wished very much to see her, she had been gone 5 weeks to the Springs.   I had heard Martha say much of her and wished much that to-morrow could come.

Next morning — Sunday — went to Meeting.   Mr. Dana of Marblehead preached ; very devout, unaffected young man ; saw not a soul I had ever seen before, excepting Mr. Grey ; thought I should not have known him as I scarcely saw his face before.   Found Mrs. Hasket Derby on my return, was disappointed in her personal appearance ; instead of finding the elegant, majestic, beautiful creature my imagination had pictured, I beheld a little, short, plump woman dressed in black, a coarse complexion and anxious eyes, yet I had not been in her company an hour without confessing to myself she was the most agreeable, fascinating woman I ever saw.   She continually pleases and delights you ; she appears to live for others, nor ever bestows a thought upon herself, yet so perfectly unconscious of it, that it seems inherent in her disposition, and to flow without any effort.   She planned parties of amusement as I was a stranger, and we fixed upon Friday for a fishing party to Nahant ; sent to Boston for some to meet us.   Monday a small party at Mrs. Derby's came to tea.   I rode in the chaise with Mr. Grey.   Mrs.

Grey and a Mr. White, an Englishman, in her carriage.
Mr. Coffin and Miss Grey in another chaise, — Mr. and
Mrs. Hasket Derby. We walked on a hill near the
house, where we had the most extensive prospect I
ever saw — the whole world seemed spread before us
covered with the richly variegated carpet of nature.
We returned home in the evening with a fine moon,
and all went to Mr. Grey's to spend the evening. Most
charming time; treated with great attention by Mrs.
Grey, who is, in my opinion, a fine woman, domestic,
fond of her children, and never so happy as in contrib-
uting to their amusement, and possesses fine sense,
animated, unceremonious, and agreeable. — Tuesday,
Doct. and Mrs. Coffin and Mrs. Sumner came down
from Boston; dined together, and all went to Hasket
Derby's farm in the afternoon. Mrs. Grey and Miss
Bishop of the party; glad to see Miss Bishop — one of
my old school-mates. Had a most charming ride; went
in the carriage with Mrs. Grey. All returned to Mr.
John Derby's and spent the evening. William Grey
and his father came in the evening; walked in the garden. — Wednesday, large party of gentlemen to dine
with Doct. Coffin. In the afternoon all went to Mrs.
Grey's; danced in the evening. Miss Bishop plays and
sings charmingly. Thursday, Doct. and Mrs. Coffin
went home, and in the afternoon went to Mrs. Hasket
Derby's with a party; every thing elegant and pleasant.
Friday to Nahant, fishing — Mr. and Mrs. Hasket
Derby, Mr. and Mrs. John Derby, Mr. and Mrs. Hersey

Derby, Miss Bishop, Mr. Grey, Mr. Coffin, and myself, Miss Heller, Mr. Prince, who looks very much like Horatio, and several others.   Met there some smart Boston beaux, — Mr. Amory Parkman, Turner, etc., etc. Spent a most charming day; caught but few fish, and very warm, yet pleasant notwithstanding — set out for home just as the sun was setting.   I returned in the chaise with William Grey, Frank with Miss Bishop, — rode 2 miles on the beach, the tide down, sun just set- ting; 'twas charming and delightful.   Saturday went out to Hersey Derby's farm to tea, went to the bathing house, summer house — and saw the Rumford[1] kitchen — elegant place, beautiful children, — rainy afternoon, we could not enjoy the pleasures of the country so well. Sunday — went to meeting and to tea with Mrs. Hasket

---

[1] The Rumford kitchen or Roaster was invented by Benjamin Thomp- son (Count Rumford), a native of Salem.   Mr. Thompson, after passing through various phases of existence, went to Bavaria, where by his powers of pleasing and wonderful inventive faculties he attracted the attention of the king, and by him was created Count Rumford.   One of Count Rum- ford's particular studies was the laws which govern heat and cold, and to him we are indebted for great improvement in our chimneys, fireplaces, and kitchen ranges.   Before his time all cooking was done over an open wood fire.   In the " Life of Count Rumford," by Ellis, page 240, we find the following : " The Roaster, if not the first, was the most simple, in- genious, and effective apparatus of the kind which, by its arrangement of flues for conveying hot air around the food in the oven as well as by econ- omizing fuel, allowed of the preparation of many articles by one fire, and greatly facilitated the labors and added to the comfort of the cook. They were especially popular in Salem, where many of the flourishing citizens had occasion to recall over their dinners the 'apprentice boy in Mr. Appleton's shop.' "

Derby; met company from Boston, — two beaux, Mr.
Lee and Mr. Davis. Monday — a party of young ladies
at Mrs. Grey's; danced in the evening, went home at
eleven, spent half an hour at Hasket Derby's on my
way; Ellen was there. Tuesday — rode out with Mrs.
Grey after dinner, returned and drank tea with Mrs.
Lambert, found company at Ellen's on my return — Mr.
and Mrs. Hasket Derby, Hersey Derby and wife, Mr.
Prince and wife, — Patty Derby that was — looks like old
Madame Milliken[1] very much. Mr. and Mrs. Hasket
Derby wish me to go to the Springs with them; know
not what to do. Ellen says go by all means, never will
have such another opportunity; she thinks my Father
and Mother would not object if I had time to write
them, which would be impossible, they go to-morrow —
what shall I do? I must go over after breakfast, I will
consult Mrs. J. Derby. I would not go for the world if
I thought my Father or Mother would not be pleased.
Mr. and Mrs. Derby go alone in their carriage. I must
think of it.

[1] Mme. Milliken, probably the daughter of John Ayer. She was the
wife of John Milliken of Boston.

Wednesday, Salem, July, 1802.

What will you say, my Dear Mother, when you find I
am gone with Mr. and Mrs. Hasket Derby to the Saratoga Springs? But I hasten to explain all. Mr. and
Mrs. Derby were going in their carriage alone. Mrs.
Derby says she never travelled without some lady, and
urged my accompanying her. I thought 'twas only a
compliment and treated it as such, but when I found she
seriously wished it and her husband joined his influence,
I began to think how it would do. I consulted Ellen
and Mr. Derby, and they both thought I ought not to
refuse an opportunity of seeing the country which perhaps may never again occur — a better one surely can
never occur. To go with Mr. and Mrs. Derby is surely
an advantage I can never hope to meet with again. Believe me, nothing would have induced me to think of
going with them unless they had been very urgent.
Ellen and Mr. Derby both say they doubt not you would
approve the plan if you were here to consult. If I did
not think so myself nothing would induce me to go —
still I regret not having it in my power to wait an
answer from you, but to-morrow afternoon we must set
out. Ellen has lent me everything necessary for my
journey, — indeed I can never repay her. She is the
most generous being I ever saw. She has nothing in
the house but is at my service, — all her handsome
dresses she wishes me to carry, indeed everything that
I can possibly want she has supplied me with. I am
glad that I shall not be compelled to purchase anything

that would be unnecessary after my return. I think I shall borrow some money of her, as it is impossible I can receive any from home, and if I do not need it, I need not spend it. You may assure yourself I shall remember to economise as much as possible. It seems as if Ellen and Mrs. Derby tried which should most oblige me. As I never determined to go till this morning, Mrs. Derby said 'twas impossible to make any new clothes, nay unnecessary, and insisted I should take any thing of hers I should want, but Ellen would not admit of that. I know not the route we shall take, but Mrs. Derby says we shall probably *go* or *return* thro' *Leicester*.[1] I shall be gratified very much at an opportunity of seeing our relations there. Ellen promises to write. I never was treated with more attention in my life. Ellen heaps me with favors, and now I have thought of this journey, she thinks she can't do enough. I intend keeping a particular journal while I am gone, which you shall all peruse on my return. We shall probably be gone four or five weeks, as it is two or three hundred miles from here. When you write me direct your letters to Salem and Mr. Derby will forward them as he will know where we are. Has Octavia returned? tell her I shall leave my Salem journal to be sent to her the first opportunity. If I go thro' Newport I shall endeavor to find out Miss Crary and Miss Clarke, and wish I had a letter from her.

And now, my dear Mother, assure me you approve of

[1] Dr. Southgate's family resided at Leicester.

my going and I shall have nothing to trouble me. **My**
Father, I think, would not object to it if I could know
his opinion.   Mr. Grey (Wm. Grey) says he is sure he
would not disapprove of it, if he knew in what good protection I was.   By-the-bye, I have received every attention from Mr. Grey's family, and Mrs. Grey is a
remarkably fine woman.   I rode out with her yesterday
afternoon, and she sent for me to go to Wexham pond
with her this afternoon ; called to excuse myself and tell
her of my projected journey ; she regretted it as I was to
have gone to Medford with her the next week, and she
had planned several parties for me which would be frus-
trated ; but she acknowledged I was perfectly right to go,
and if 'twas her daughter she should be much gratified
at the opportunity.   Mr. and Mrs. Derby say I must tell
you they will take good *care* of me and they shall take
the full protection of me.   Write me soon, or request
my Father or Octavia ; but pray if you disapprove, do
not tell me till I return, 'twill be too late to alter or re-
tract, and I should be wretched if I thought you disapproved my going, — do write, or ask my Father, I shall
feel uneasy.   My love to all friends, and believe me, with
great affection,   Your   Eliza.

Francestown (New Hampshire),
July 26, 1802.

My dear Father :

   My letter in which I informed you of my intended
journey, my motives for it, etc., you will receive before

this, I therefore think it unnecessary to say any more, but rest with full confidence on the indulgent heart of an affectionate Father, who I trust knows my heart too well to think me capable of acting in opposition to what I know to be his wishes. We left Salem on Thursday evening and slept at Ten hills in Charleston, breakfasted in Webrion,[1] and dined in Betavia.[2] We had a fine view of the celebrated Middlesex canal, which in future ages must do honor to our country, — such monuments of industry and perseverance raise our opinion of our countrymen; it will be 25 miles in length when completed, running from Deckel[3] to Medford river, — the river of Concord supplies it with water, boats pass every day, and parties of pleasure are always sailing on it. In my journal I have been more particular, here I say but little as we are in a miserable tavern and the horses almost ready. I cannot tell you the route we are going, — Mr. Derby's motive is to see the most pleasant part of the country that he has not seen before. From Bilusia we came through Chelmsford, Inigsborough where old Irving lived and Miss Pitts, now Mrs. Brimby, the heiress of his fortune has a most elegant tasty country house on the banks of the Merrimack — which forms a most beautiful scene in front of the house and gives a full view of the river in each direction, — more of this in my journal. We are on a new turnpike road, from Amherst to Dartmouth. We shall go up to Dartmouth College as 'tis wholly a jaunt of pleasure, and Mr. Derby

---

[1] Woburn.   [2] Billerica.   [3] Dracut.

is determined to be in no haste, to enquire everything
worth seeing and not to mind 6 or 7 miles from a direct
road, — they are very attentive to me and have gone a
mile from the direct road to show me something they
had seen before.   Mr. Derby has been such a traveller
that he is now one of the most useful travelling companions in the world; his wife is the most engaging, unaffected, family woman in the world, and instead of feeling myself a burden to them, they make me feel of the
utmost consequence.   We passed thro' several pretty villages on coming here — tho' it is almost a new country,
scarcely cleared up, — excepting a small village every 6
or 7 miles; the most hilly, mountainous, woody country
I ever was in, — here as I look round me I see nothing
but enormous high hills, covered with trees and almost
mingling with the clouds.   One of them in particular —
Francestown [1] is about 12 miles from Amherst, a number of pleasant houses and a very elegant meeting-
house, — how different from our part of the country! —
here, if there is but one handsome house in town there
will be a meeting house.   I have passed but one on my
journey, in these new back places, but what was painted
and a steeple!   From Dartmouth we go down to
Northampton and then to Lebanon Springs, then to
Ballstown and Saratoga, and return by the way of New
Haven, Hartford, etc.   I shall have a fine opportunity
of seeing the country on Connecticut River.   Mr.
Derby does not know the route he shall go, but shall

---

[1] *Francestown*, named so after Gov. Wentworth's wife.

depend on what he hears; we shall go thro' a part of
the States of Vermont, Connecticut, and New York, so
that in our tour we shall be in 5 different States.   I
shall write very often, and wish you, my Dear Father, to
write me by the return of the mail, and direct to Pittsfield in Massachusetts, — or to Mr. John Derby in Salem.   If we go thro' Leicester I shall find out our relations.   Tell Octavia and Horatio I shall write them
soon, but as I keep a particular journal which they shall
all see, 'tis not so material.   I hear the carriage — love
to all.   ELIZA.

                                Ballston Springs, August 22, 1802.

My Dearest Mother :

I feel at this moment as if I could fly ! so far from
home, received no letters, yet at Albany I expect to
find them, let me at least hope what 'twill delight me so
much to realize.   I sometimes almost fear to receive a
letter from home, — yet my indulgent Parents will pardon the liberty I took in coming this journey, as I trust
they are convinced by my past life, that I would not for
the universe act in opposition to what I knew they approved.   I am convinced when you know Mr. and Mrs.
Derby you will feel that I was both secure and honored
in their protection.   I cannot tell you half I owe them,
never in my life was I treated with more affectionate
attention.   They appear as much interested in all I do
as if I were their daughter.   You know my heart, my

dearest Mother, you know it never was insensible to the smallest favor, what then must be its sensation when it is thus overpowered by affectionate kindness. I long to convince them how much I feel, but words are inadequate. My Father has seen Mr. D., I wish he would write to him, I think it would be no more than just to thank him for the care he has taken of his daughter. It seems as if he had a right to expect something of the kind. They are the finest couple I know of, so different from what I expected to find them. I thought Mr. Derby a gay gallant man like Mr. Davis, but he is a plain, noble-hearted, sincere, generous man, — talks very little and one of the pleasantest dispositions in the world. In Mrs. Derby I thought to find a gay woman of fashion, but not a soul that ever knew her could help loving her. I never saw a person so universally beloved. We have been here at Ballston a fortnight to-morrow. It has been one continued scene of idleness and dissipation — have a ball every other night, ride, walk, stroll about the piazzas, dress, — indeed we do nothing that seems like improvement. But still I think there is no place where one may study the different characters and dispositions to greater advantage. You meet here the most genteel people from every part of our country, — ceremony is thrown off and you are acquainted very soon. You may select those you please for intimates, and among so many you certainly will find some agreeable, amiable companions. For a week we sat down at the table every day with 60 or 70 persons, to-day we were all speak-

ing of the latter being very thin because we had only
40. There are as many more at the other boarding
house, continually going and coming, and now there is
scarcely 10 persons here that were here when we came.
We went last week to *Lake George*, about 40 miles from
here, — made up a party and went on Tuesday, breakfasted at *Saratoga*, where the Springs formerly most
celebrated were, and dined about 14 miles this side the
lake, at the most beautiful place I ever saw. Perhaps
you have heard of Glens-Falls ; they are said to exceed in *beauty* the Falls of *Niagara* — tho' in *sublimity*
must fall far short. I never imagined anything so picturesque, sublime and beautiful as the scenery around
this enchanting place. The rocks on the shores have
exactly the appearance of elegant, magnificent ruins,
they are entirely of *slate*, and seem piled in regular
forms with shrubs and grass growing in between. I
looked around me for an hour and I every moment discovered something new to admire, — nothing could exceed the beautiful variety of the scenery. I left this
elegant place with painful regret. About sunset we
came in view of the *Lake*, it is a most beautiful sheet of
water, Morse says 36 miles long and from one to 7
broad, full of beautiful Islands, 365 in all and of every
size and shape. It is surrounded by very high hills and
mountains rising one above the other in majestic grandeur. In the morning we went out to fish, sailed about
4 miles on the lake to a little Island where we went on
shore, — nothing could exceed the beautiful grandeur of

the prospect; we anchored off, — I found it very charming fishing, the water so perfectly transparent that we could see the fish swimming around the dock. Our first intention was to sail down the lake to Lake Champlain and visit the ruins of the fortifications at Ticonderoga, but some of our party dissuaded us from it. We saw the ruins of Fort George and the bloody pond — where so many poor wretches were thrown. We stopt on our return at the field where Burgoyne surrendered his army; it is now covered with corn and nothing to distinguish it from the surrounding fields ; we returned by a different route, for 10 miles we rode directly on the banks of the Hudson river, nothing could be more delightful, our road wound with the river which was beautifully overhung with trees ; we returned here Thursday night, found them dancing. I joined, and the next night we had a ball at the other house ; there again I danced till 12 o'clock and the next morning got up quite sick, — to-day I am finely again and have made a resolution not to dance again whilst I stay here. This all think I can't keep, but they shall see I can. Col. Boyd came here last week but went away while we were gone to Lake George — to Canada I believe. He says you had not heard of my coming when he left Portland, so he could tell me nothing new. We shall probably leave here on Tuesday or Wednesday, stay at Albany a few days and go to Lebanon again, perhaps to Williamston Commencement. We are engaged to spend the day at Mr. Ransalaers, the former L Governor, and one at Mr.

THE VAN RENSSELAER MANOR HOUSE

Ransalaers — his brother, who is Mayor of the City. I know not how long 'twill be before we return to Salem, but I really begin to think of home with a great deal of anxiety. Tell Octavia I never go into the Ball room to dance without wishing for her; how delighted should I be if Horatio and Octavia were here with me! How charming will it be when I get home again! Believe me, my Dear Mother, I shall love home more than ever. I long to sit me down by the instrument some evening after the business of the day is over, with you, my Father, and all round me, or to hear Octavia sing and play. This scene of dissipation may please for a while by its novelty, but it soon satiates — no regular employment, I have never been in the habit of spending my time in idleness; and they say here that the Southern ladies seem more at home here than the Northern ladies and do not appear to think industry necessary to happiness. I hope to find many letters at Albany. I have kept a regular journal which will assist my memory in relating my adventures, when I return home again. I wrote Horatio last week and told him to send the letter home for you to read. I look forward to returning with the greatest pleasure. I suppose you are fixed upon a house and will move by the time I return, let me know as I am anxious to hear about it. Give my best love to all my friends and tell Octavia I have more to say to her than I can gabble in a month. Oh I long to get home again. I find no time to write, if I lock myself in my chamber I have so many knocks at the door — Miss

Southgate go and walk— go down to the spring — somebody wants you below, — so many interruptions, 'tis almost impossible.   After I retire for the night I am so
tired and sleepy and my chamber is so hot, I *cannot*
write ; 'tis Sunday to-day (tho' all days are alike here)
and I have determined I would write home.   I wonder
how it was possible for Martha to write so much, — I
hear of her from all the Southern people, they all speak
in raptures.   Give my love to Mrs. Coffin and kiss all
the children — Mamy particularly, what would I give to
hear her open my door and run in this moment.   Mrs.
Derby says I get low-spirited when I write home, the
only way is to think as little of it as possible whilst I am
so far off.   I shall write again from Albany, where I
hope to find letters.

Ever your affectionate   ELIZA.

To the care of Robert Southgate,
    Scarborough,
       (District of Maine.)

Albany, August 8, 1802.

Thus far, my dear Ellen, have we proceeded without
any thing to mortify or disappoint us ; I wrote you the
night I arrived at Lebanon, the next morning the bell
rang and we all assembled to breakfast ; there were about
thirty ladies, much dressed, looking very handsome, it
seemed more like a ball room than a breakfasting room.
We were the last that came in, and all eyes were fixed
upon us.   Lady Nesbert and the Allston family from

Carolina were opposite. This daughter of Col. Burr is a little, smart - looking woman, very *learned* they say, understands the dead languages — not pedantic, rather reserved — Lady Nesbert,[1] a most interesting woman, full black eyes with a wild melancholy expression and a voice so sweet and plaintive, you would think it melancholy music. I never heard her speak a dozen times since I have been here and rarely ever smile. Old Mrs. Allston, the mother, is a *sour-looking* woman, nothing affable or condescending. Miss Allston, they say, is a romp, though her mother restrains her so much you would not suspect it. Old Mr. Allston [2] is affable and agreeable. We had likewise there a Mr. Constable [3] of N. Y.; has lived in great style, — very much the gentleman.

Miss Ashley from N. Y. whom I mentioned in my last is a truly *fashionable* City Belle. She is a fortune, but I believe not of family. The Gentleman she calls her father and whose name she takes 'tis said was hired by a British officer, her real father, to marry the mother and adopt the daughter, and a very large sum was given him. He appears an abandoned old rake, pale and sallow. Oh! he is a horrid-looking object, in a deep consumption I imagine; she is very attentive. But, good heavens!

[1] Lady Nesbert, wife of Sir John Nesbert, celebrated for a race ridden against John Randolph in 1719.

[2] Joseph Allston, of South Carolina, had married, February 2, 1801, Theodosïa Burr, only daughter of Aaron Burr.

[3] This was Mr. William Constable, who married, February 26, 1810, Miss Mary Elizabeth McVickar, daughter of John McVickar, Esq.

Ellen, I had no idea of a fashionable girl before — one that devotes her whole attention to fashion. I have much to tell you when I return, about the Miss Ashleys' french style of dress. Mr. and Mrs. Ransselear[1] left Lebanon the day before we did with Mr. and Miss Westelo,[2] Mr. Welsh,[3] the Miss Stevensons, and Miss Livingston the Albany Belle, — all belong to Albany. Mr. and Miss Westelo, Miss Beakman, and Mr. Ransselear, who is Mayor of the City, called last evening and we all went to walk — went into Miss Westelo's and spent a charming hour; all returned with us, and we engaged to go to meeting with Mr. and Miss Westelo and take tea at the Mayor's this afternoon. Mr. Westelo is going to Balston in company with us and a Mr. Kane[4] of N. Y. whom we met at the Coffee House — very genteel man. Another little lawyer from Litchfield, who came in from Lebanon with us, is likewise, on Monday; so we shall

[1] The Patroon Stephen Van Rensselaer had lately married his second wife, Cornelia Patterson. Miss Southgate spelt the name as it was then usually pronounced.

[2] Rensselaer Westerlo and his sister Catherine Westerlo, who afterwards married Mr. Woodworth. Their mother was Catherine Livingston, oldest daughter of Philip, commonly known as the "Signer," he having been one of the signers of the Declaration of Independence. Miss Livingston had first married Stephen Van Rensselaer, Patroon of the Manor, and by him had had three children: Stephen, who succeeded his father ; Philip, mayor of the city of Albany ; and a daughter. Mrs. Van Rensselaer remarried Dominie Westerlo.

[3] Walsh (?).

[4] Oliver Kane, a merchant of New York. He married, at Providence, Rhode Island, May 22, 1803, Miss Ann Eliza Clarke, daughter of John Innes Clarke.

have a very pleasant party. Mr. Kane says I shall meet one of their genteelest N. Y. beaux at Balston, Mr. Bowne. I wonder if it is the same I have heard you mention. I shall find out. About eleven o'clock, or rather twelve, I was surprised by some delightful music; a number of instruments, and most elegantly playing " Rise ! Cynthia ! rise ! " I jumped up and by the light of the moon saw five gentlemen under the window. To Mr. Westelo I suppose we are indebted. " Washington March," " Blue Bells of Scotland," " Taste Life's glad moments," " Boston March," and many other charming tunes — played most delightfully. I have heard no music since I left Salem till this, and I was really charmed. The bell will ring soon and I must finish this after meeting. — Sunday afternoon. The dinner was brought on the table just as the bell rang for meeting, so that we were obliged to stay at home this afternoon, and tell Mr. Westelo and his sister, who called again for me, as Mrs. Derby did not go out, that I would go to Mrs. Ranselear's after meeting. In the morning, Mr. Derby and myself went to the New Dutch Church with Mr. and Miss Westelo and sat with them next pew to the Patroon's, whom you saw in Salem with his beautiful wife.

After meeting, Mr. Westelo came with the Patroon and his wife to see us. She is really beautiful, dressed very plain ; cotton cambric morning gown, white sarsnet cloak, hair plain, and black veil thrown carelessly over her head. They urged our dining there to-morrow, but Mr. Derby is determined to set out in the morning for

Balston — the waters, all tell him, will be of great service — when we return we shall go and see them.   A great number of elegant gentlemen are here in this house, many from N. Y., some going to the springs.   Your Boston Mr. Amory and Mr. Lee would look rusty long side them.   Hush, not a word! — Mr. Kane of N. Y., whose sister married Robert Morris, is here, will set out for the springs in company with us, Mr. Westelo and some others.   We shall go to Lake George and probably make a party from Balston.   Mrs. Derby has insisted on my wearing the sarsnet dress to-day as we shall drink tea at the Mayor's, where the Patroon and wife will probably be.   I am every moment reminded of your affectionate kindness, which I hope never to be insensible to.

You wrote Mamma, I suppose.   I have not received a line from anybody ; shall depend on finding letters at Pittsfield or Lebanon ; do write me everything.   I have so much to tell you that I cannot write.   Mrs. Derby, I cannot tell you how much I owe her.   She treats me with so much affection, and she says she believes Mr. Derby feels as much interest in me as if I were his daughter — wishes everything I wear should be becoming, and indeed they both treat me with all the attention and affection my most sanguine expectation could desire.   I do not wish to be treated with more affection ; think then, dear Ellen ! how sensibly I must feel it, how gratifying to my feelings.   I can never forget the obligation I owe to you and them.   My best love to your husband ; tell

him when I return I shall have a whole world of news
for him. I long to hear from you, do write soon. At
Balston I will write again. Many people will be talking
about my going this journey; many will censure me
perhaps; if you, dear Ellen, should hear any of their ill-
natured remarks you could not do me a greater favor
than to vindicate my conduct. I have never for one moment since I left Salem regretted I came. The affectionate attention of Mr. and Mrs. Derby delights my
very heart, 'twas more than I had a right to expect. I
have received much delight in this tour, seen much elegant company, variety of character and manners. I am
sensible it will be a source of great improvement, as well
as pleasure. I shall have seen that style and splendor,
which has so many magic charms when viewed at a distance, divested of its false place, we find it mingled with
as many pains as any other situation in life, nay, more
poignant pain. I feel that I shall not be at all injured
by this life; though I enjoy myself highly and mingle
with these people with much delight, I shall return happy
and content. Mr. Derby is quite unwell, has taken
nothing but milk since we left Salem, his stomach re-
fuses everything else. I have strong hopes that the
Balston waters will have a good effect. Everyone tells
him so. A gentleman just from Balston says there is a
great deal of company at the Springs, dance every other
night. If the waters agree with Mr. Derby we shall
stay a week or ten days. I have written home a number of times, which together with my journal take up all

my leisure time, and that is stolen from the hrs. devoted
to sleep.   I would give anything for one line from you
this moment.   How delighted I shall be when I return!
Any news from Martha?   If any letter arrives for me
send it on to Pittsfield.   How charming it would be if
we were all together going to the Springs!   I have not
time to write anything about Albany fine society — I
believe full of Dutch houses.   Adieu, love to all friends.

Mrs. Eleanor Coffin.   ELIZA.

                                    Salem, September 9, 1802.

My Dearest Mother:

   Once more I am safe in Salem and my first thoughts
turn toward home.   I arrived last night.   The attention I have received from Mr. and Mrs. Derby has
been of a kind that I shall look forward with delight to
a time when I may be able to return it as I wish.   I
am in perfect health and spirits and have enjoyed the
journey more than I can express to you.   I don't know
that I have had an unpleasant hour since I have been
gone, and what is still more pleasing, I look back on
every scene without regret or pain.   At Leicester I
went to Uncle Southgate's, and Cousin William helped
me into the carriage when I left the tavern the next
morning.   We did not return thro' North-Hampton,
and I consequently missed seeing Aunt Dickenson.   I
regret it extremely, but Mr. Derby was in such haste
to return, that he left us at Worcester and took the

stage. I therefore could not say a word of Hadley. I found two letters from Octavia on my return here; felt really grieved at Eliza Wait's death; she must feel it sensibly as they were such intimate friends, yet time blunts the sharp pangs of affection, and when I return she will feel that happiness has only fled for a while to make its return more delightful. I have received more attentions at the Springs than in my whole life before, I know not why it was, but I went under every advantage. Mr. Derby is so well known and respected, and they are such charming people and treated me with so much affection, it could not be otherwise! Among the many gentlemen I have become acquainted and who have been attentive, one I believe is serious. I know not, my dearest Mother, how to introduce this subject, yet as I fear you may hear it from others and feel anxious for my welfare, I consider it a duty to tell you all. At Albany, on our way to Ballston, we put up at the same house with a *Mr. Bowne* from New York; he went on to the Springs the same day we did, and from that time was particularly attentive to me; he was always of our parties to ride, went to Lake George in company with us, and came on to Lebanon when we did, — for 4 weeks I saw him every day and probably had a better opportunity of knowing him than if I had seen him as a common acquaintance in town for years. I felt cautious of encouraging his attentions, tho' I did not wish to *discourage* it, — there were so many *New Yorkers* at the Springs who knew him perfectly

that I easily learnt his character and reputation ; he
is a man of *business*, uniform in his conduct and *very
much respected;* all this we knew from report. Mr.
and Mrs. Derby were very much pleased with him,
but conducted towards me with peculiar *delicacy*, left
me entirely to myself, as on a subject of so much
importance they scarcely dared give an opinion. I
left myself in a situation truly embarrassing. At such
a distance from all my friends, — my Father and
Mother a perfect stranger to the person, — and pre-
possessed in his favor as much as so short an acquaintance would sanction, — his conduct was such as I shall
ever reflect on with the greatest pleasure, — open, candid, generous, and delicate. He is a man in whom I
could place the most unbounded confidence, nothing
rash or impetuous in his disposition, but weighs ma-
turely every circumstance ; he knew I was not at liberty to encourage his addresses without the approbation of my Parents, and appeared as solicitous that I
should act with strict propriety as one of my most dis-
interested friends. He advised me like a friend and
would not have suffered me to do anything improper.
He only required I would not discourage his addresses
till he had an opportunity of making known to my Parents his character and wishes — this I promised and
went so far as to tell him I approved him as far as I
knew him, but the decision must rest with my Parents,
their wishes were my law. He insisted upon coming
on immediately : that I absolutely refused to consent to.

MR. WALTER BOWNE.

Miniature by Malbone.

ARTOTYPE, E. BIERSTADT, N. Y.

But all my persuasion to wait till winter had no effect; the first of October he *will come.* I could not prevent it without a positive *refusal;* this I felt no disposition to give. And now, my dearest Mother, I submit myself wholly to the wishes of my Father and you, convinced that my happiness is your warmest wish, and to promote it has ever been your study. That I feel deeply interested in Mr. Bowne I candidly acknowledge, and from the knowledge I have of his heart and character I think him better calculated to promote my happiness than any person I have yet seen; he is a firm, steady, serious man, nothing light or trifling in his character, and I have every reason to think he has well weighed his sentiments towards me, — nothing rash or premature. I have referred him wholly to you, and you, my dearest Parents, must decide. Octavia mentioned nothing about moving, but I am extremely anxious to know how soon we go into Portland and what house we shall have. Write me immediately on the subject, and let me know if you approve my conduct. Mr. Bowne wishes me to remain here until he comes on and then let him carry me home: this I objected to, but will depend on your advice. I shall be obliged to stay a few weeks longer, — Harriet Howards expects me a week in Cambridge, Mrs. Sumner a week in Boston, and Mrs. Hasket Derby another week. I am now with Ellen and shall stay till Mrs. Coffin comes up, then according to promise go to Mrs. Lucy Derby's. I feel extremely anxious to hear you have moved into town, and shall most probably be here until then; write me immediately. If you wish any furniture, Mrs. Sumner will assist me in purchasing whatever you wish. I mentioned in my letter, when I set out on this journey I borrowed 15 dollars of Ellen; I wish you to send it to me immediately after receiving this, if you have not already sent it. I shall likewise stand in need of a little, as I have unavoidably incurred many expenses in this journey which I should not otherwise have done. Mr. Derby has loaded me with obligations, all my expenses he defrayed as if I was his daughter, and in such a manner as endears him more than I can express. You cannot imagine how interested they both are in the subject I have been writing you upon, — my nearest friends cannot feel more, they have witnessed the whole progress, and if you knew them, would be convinced they would not have let me act improperly, they both approve my conduct. I wish my Father would write to Mr. Derby and know what he says of Mr. B.'s character. I don't know but 'tis a subject too delicate to give his opinion, but I can conceive that my Father might request it without any impropriety; and do, my Dear Mother, beg him to say any thing in his power to convince him that we all feel sensibly their great attention to me. You know not how anxious I feel for my Father to write him something of that kind, not that they appear to expect it, but on the contrary insist that they have been more obliged than I have, and really seem to think so; but this rather strengthens than lessens the obligation, nothing should have induced me to receive such from people who felt they were conferring favors. I long to hear when we move into Portland, *do* write me. My best love to Horatio and Octavia, and tell them I shall write as soon as possible. I found a large packet of 5 sheets from Martha, dated Paris, June 28th ; tells me every thing, speaks almost in raptures of Buonaparte, says Uncle Rufus has a little son [1] about 12 years old at school there, one of the finest boys she ever saw. I find most of the Southern people whom we met at the Springs, think Uncle Rufus stands as good a chance of being President as any one spoken of. I have listened for hours to his praises when not one knew how much I was interested ; it was known from Mrs. Derby I was his niece, and it really gave me great consequence. I thought of Mrs. Dewitt and laughed. Judge Sedgwick told me had letters from him as late as June, and that he was determined on returning in the Spring. I long to hear from home. My love to all my friends, and believe me, with every sentiment of *duty* and *affection,*   Your daughter   ELIZA.

Martha sent me a most elegant Indispensable, white lutestring spangled with silver, and a beautiful bracelet for the arm made of her hair ; she is too good — to love me as she says, more than ever.

[1] James G. King.

Portland, Nov. — Friday, — 1802.

Mr. Davis is going on to Boston and will have a letter for you. I am delighted to hear that Mamma is better. I send you some of Miss Homer's wedding cake; married on Monday. You say Rufus Emerson has returned and tells them a great many stories; when you write next tell me what he says, and where he heard, and all about it, for everything interests me. Mr. Bowne has not arrived, I am out of all patience, cannot imagine what detains him, — 4 weeks to-morrow since he took Mr. Codman's letter. These Quakers are governed by such a *slow spirit* — I wish the deuce had them. I shall be really uneasy if he don't come soon. I want some *money*, my last dollar I gave Horatio to buy Mamma's *oranges*. I have written to Mrs. Derby to buy me a *winter gown ;* in her last she says she has bought it but does not mention the price. I wish the money to send to her soon as I hear ; a little likewise for occasional expenses, 'tis not pleasant to be without. I have been in but one party since Mamma's sickness; shall certainly not go out more than I can possibly avoid. Mrs. Derby is quite out at Mr. B.'s not coming. I'll not be so ungenerous as to condemn him without giving an opportunity of vindicating himself, some circumstances I know not of may detain him. All our friends are well. Send me the money as soon as possible ; and don't forget to tell particularly what Rufus says, whom he saw, what they told him, and when he heard all. In some cases trifles acquire importance — mole hills become mountains. Adieu. Eliza.

Love to Mamma, and tell her I am out of all patience.
Miss Octavia Southgate.

Boston, May 30, 1803.

Here we are, my dear Octavia, at Mrs. Carter's Boarding House, and tho' we have endeavored to keep ourselves as much out of the way as possible, a great many people have called to pay their respects to Mr. and Mrs. Bowne. The first person we met driving thro' Salem was Mr. *Lee* just coming in town ; he bowed very low and pass'd. We went to a public house and had not been there 3 minutes before Mr. Lee came in determined to be the first to call on us ; he shook hands very cordially, congratulated us, and went with us up to Ellen's. We promised to drive with Ellen, and went to see Mrs. H. Derby; spent a charming hour and returned to Ellen's, dined, and all went to Lucy Derby's to tea, Mr. Lee and a dozen others. Mr. Bowne and myself called on Mrs. Grey, and after a very pleasant day returned to Ellen's and stayed the night, and the next morning, which was Wednesday, came into Boston, — 'twas *election day* and all the world was in motion. I could not bear to come to Mrs. Carter's, but Mr. Bowne thought he ought to. Mr. Lee got to Boston as soon as we did and came immediately to see us and offer his services; he has been here again this morning and is going to ride into the country with us to show us some fine seats. Doctor

Boice, Mr. Davis, Mr. Cabot, Charles Bradbury, Tom
Coffin and a dozen other gentlemen, whose names I
have forgot, and who came with the Miss Lowells and
Miss Russells. We have prevented all invitations on,
by constantly saying we were going out of town immediately. Mr. Lee insisted, when I expressed a wish to
see Miss *Wyre*, on letting her know I was in town, — he
went and she came immediately back. I was very glad
to see her and she appeared so herself at seeing me.
Some ladies and gentlemen came in; and after they were
gone, Alicia, Mr. B. and myself went a-shopping; — the
fashions for bonnets, Octavia, are very ugly; Alicia had
a large, white glazed cambric one made without paste-
board. But I have not told you how Gen. Knox [1] found
us out at Newburyport. We always kept by ourselves,
but in passing the entry Gen'l Knox, who had just come
in the stage, met Mr. B. and asked where he was from
— (Mr. Bowne kept here with Mrs. Carter when Gen'l
Knox was here last winter); he told him from the Eastward. — Alone? — no. — Who is with you? — *Mrs. Bowne.*
So plump a question he could not evade, so the General
insisted on being introduced to the bride. I was walk-

[1] General Henry Knox was a general in the American army during
the Revolution. He entered it at the beginning of the war as a captain of
the Boston Grenadiers. He was the first Secretary of War of the United
States. He married the daughter of Secretary Flucker. General and
Mrs. Knox grew to be enormously stout and were perhaps the largest
couple in the city of New York at the time when Washington was inau-
gurated as first President of the United States. General Knox's home
was at Thomaston, Maine.

ing the room and reading, perfectly unsuspicious, when
the opening of the door and Mr. Bowne's voice—"Gen'l
Knox, my love," quite roused me; he came up, took my
hand very gracefully, pres't it to his lips and begged leave
to congratulate me on the event that had lately taken
place. After a few minutes' conversation — "And
pray, sir," said he, turning to Mr. Bowne — "when did
this happy event take place?" I felt my face glow, but
Mr. Bowne, always delicate and collected, said — "'Tis
not a fortnight since, Sir." The stage drove to the door,
and after hoping to see us at Mrs. Carter's he took his
leave, and this morning — (he was out all day yesterday)
— I found him waiting in the breakfast room to see me.
He introduced me to General Pinckney [1] and his family
from Carolina, — Gen'l Pinckney, they say, is to be our
next President. "*Mr. Bowne*," said Gen'l Knox to Gen.
P., "has done us the honor to come to the District of
Maine for a bud to transplant in New York." He was
very polite and said "he must find us out in New York."
Only think, I never thought of the *wedding-cake* when I
was at Salem. You would laugh to hear "*Mrs. Bowne*"
and "Miss Southgate" all in a breath — "How do you
do, Miss Southgate?" — "I beg pardon, *Mrs. Bowne*,"
and do it on purpose I believe; when I hear an old acquaintance call me "Mrs. Bowne" it really makes me
stare at first, it sounds so very odd. Mr. B. will be in,

---

[1] General Pinckney of South Carolina had served in the American
army. He had two daughters, one of whom married Col. Francis K.
Huger.

in a moment — and if I don't seal my letter, he will insist on seeing it, so love to all.   I depend on finding
letters at New Haven.   I have a thousand things to
say, — (some ladies enquire for Mrs. Bowne, so says the
servant, — I'll tell you who they are when I come up,)
— Mrs. Bartlett and Alicia; they insist on our taking tea
and spending the evening; we promised if we did not
leave town after dinner that we would.   Adieu, adieu.
Mr. Bowne sends a great deal of love.

Your affectionate sister,

Eliza Bowne.

New Haven, June 1, 1803.

Your letter, my dear Octavia, was the first thing to
welcome me on my arrival at this City.   I cannot describe to you my sensations when it came.   I can rarely
think of home without more pain than pleasure, and yet
if there is a being on earth perfectly *blest* 'tis your sister
Eliza.   How infinitely more happy than when I left you.
You cannot imagine how delightful has been our journey.
We have stop't at every pleasant place, enjoyed all the
beauties of the Spring in the richest and most luxuriant
country I ever saw.   I wrote you last from Boston. —
The afternoon following Mr. Lee called to accompany us
a few miles out of town ; he had requested Mr. Lyman's
permission to go out to his seat in Waltham that Mr.
Bowne and myself might have an opportunity to see it,
as it is the most beautiful place round Boston.   We set

THE LYMAN PLACE—WALTHAM

out about 4 o'clock — had a most charming ride. Mr.
Lee was remarkably sociable, attentive and polite, both
to Mr. Bowne and myself. He talks just as sociably,
and called me "Miss Southgate" and "Mrs. B." all in a
breath as fast as he could talk. I have no time to tell
you of this elegant place of Mr. Lyman's, great taste in
laying out the grounds. It surpasses everything of the
kind I ever saw; beautiful serpentine river or brook
thickly planted with trees, and elegant swans swimming
about — you can't imagine — 'twas almost like enchantment. After Mr. Lee had gathered me a bouquet large
enough to supply a ballroom — of the most elegant and
rare flowers, — full blown roses — buds — everything
beautiful, we jumped into the carriage, he shook us cordially by the hand, wished us every happiness, and hoped
to see us in New York ere long. Sunday morning we
got to Springfield, stayed the day, it recalled so many
pleasing sensations. When we parted there — how
different were our feelings — our happiness was aug-
mented by the contrast. From Springfield to Hartford
was charming; much pleased with Hartford, stayed a
day and night there. From Hartford to New Haven
is the most elegant ride you can possibly imagine, — a
fine turnpike about 30 miles, and such a picturesque,
rich, luxuriant country, such variety and beauty — oh
'twas charming! Mr. Bowne is waiting for me this full
hour to walk in the Mall, — What shall I do, he hurries
so? Well, I never saw a place so charming as New
Haven; we have been all over it, — visited the College,

everything, and I give it the preference to any place I know of — a particular description I defer. I have no time to say a word of your letter; write me immediately on receiving this to New York, where we shall be on Saturday. Mr. Bowne's best love with mine to all the family. Adieu — I have ten thousand things more to say but can't. Write me immediately.

Ever your affectionate

ELIZA BOWNE.

New York, June 6, 1803.

I sit down to catch a moment to tell you all I have to before another interruption. I have so much to say, where shall I begin — my head is most turned, and yet I am very happy; I am enraptured with New York. You cannot imagine anything half so beautiful as *Broadway*, and I am sure you would say I was more romantic than ever if I should attempt to describe the Battery, — the elegant water prospect, — you can have no idea how refreshing in a warm evening. The gardens we have not yet visited; indeed we have so many delightful things 'twill take me forever; and my husband declares he takes as much pleasure in showing them to me as I do in seeing them; you would believe it if you saw him. Did I tell you anything of Brother John? handsome young man, great literary taste; he is one of the family; nothing of the appearance of a Quaker. Mrs. King, another sister, they all say looks like me. Mrs. Murray,

who is very sick now, has a daughter, a charming, lively
girl, about 19, and the little witch introduced me in a
laughing way last night to some of her friends as *Aunt
Eliza*. I protest against that ; her brother Robert 17
years old too ; I positively must declare off from being
Aunt to them. Caroline and I went a shopping yesterday, and 'tis a fact that the little white satin quaker bonnets, cap-crowns, are the most fashionable that are worn
— lined with pink or blue or white ; but I'll not have
one, for if any of my old acquaintance should meet me
in the street they would laugh, I would if I were them.
I mean to send sister Boyd a quaker cap, the first tasty
one I see ; Caroline's are too plain, but she has promised
to get me a more fashionable pattern.   'Tis the fashion.
I see nothing new or pretty, — large sheer muslin shawls
put on as Sally Weeks wears hers are much worn, they
show the form thro' and look pretty; silk nabobs,
plaided, colored and white, are much worn, very short
waists, hair very plain. Maria Denning has been to see
me, I was very happy, — several spring acquaintance.
Expect Eliza Watts and Jane every moment, they did
not know where I was to be found. Last night we were
at the play — "The way to get married." Mr. Hodgkinson [1] in *Tangent* is inimitable. Mrs. Johnson a sweet,

---

[1] Hodgkinson made his first appearance in New York as *Vapid*. He
was born in Manchester, England, 1767; his father was an innkeeper named
Meadowcraft. Young Meadowcraft ran away from home, took the
name of Hodgkinson, and joined the stage. His wife, to whom he was
married on his arrival in America, by Bishop Moore, was Miss Brett of

interesting actress in Julia, and Jefferson,[1] a great comic player, were all that were particularly pleasing; house was very thin so late in the season.   Mr. and Mrs. Codman [2] came to see me.   I should have known her in a moment from her resemblance to Ellen and the family, — appeared very happy to see me, — Mr. Codman was happy, Mrs. Codman would now have somebody to call her friend, etc., etc.   Maria Denning told me Uncle Rufus [King] was expected every day; we have such contradictory accounts, we hardly know what to believe. As to housekeeping, we don't begin to talk anything of it yet.   Mr. Bowne says not till October, however you shall hear all our plans.   I anticipate so much happiness; I am sure if any body ought to I may.   My heart is *full* sometimes when I think how much more blest I am than most of the world.   At this moment there is not a single circumstance presents itself to my mind that I feel unpleasant to reflect on: the sweet tranquillity of my feelings — so different from any thing I ever before felt — such a confidence — my every feeling reciprocated and every wish anticipated. — I write to

the Bath Theatre. She died in New York of consumption, September, 1803. Mr. and Mrs. Hodgkinson received $100 a week for their services, which was the highest amount yet paid to any two performers in America.

[1] This Joseph Jefferson was the grandfather of the present Joseph Jefferson.

[2] Mr. and Mrs. William Codman. Mrs. Codman was a Miss Coffin. William Codman had at that time an insurance office at No. 28 South Street, New York.

you what would appear singular to any other. — You can easily imagine my feelings. — I see Mr. B. now where he is universally known and respected, and every hour see some new proof how much he is honored and esteemed here; the most gratifying to the heart you can imagine, cannot but make an impression on mine. We talk of you when we get to housekeeping, how delightful 'twill be — what a sweet domestic circle! — I must leave you; Caty says — "Mrs. Walter (for so the servants call me to distinguish), a gentleman below wishes to see you." Adieu. Who can this said gentleman be?

Mr. Rodman was below, whom I saw at the Springs, and for these two hours there has been so many calling I thought I should never get up to finish my letter. Mrs. Henderson,[1] whom I mentioned to you as one of the most elegant women in New York, and Maria Denning, her sister, came in soon after. Engaged to Mrs. Henderson's for Friday.

Thursday Morning: — I have been to two of the Gardens, Columbia,[2] near the Battery, a most romantic beautiful place; 'tis enclosed in a circular form and little rooms and boxes all around, with tables and chairs, these full of company; the trees all interspersed with lamps twinkling thro' the branches; in the centre a

---

[1] Mrs. Henderson and Miss Denning were daughters of William Denning, a well-known New York merchant.

[2] *Columbia Gardens* were on the corner of Broadway and Prince Street.

pretty little building with a fountain playing continually, the rays of the lamps on the drops of water gave it a cool sparkling appearance that was delightful. This little building, which has a kind of canopy and pillars all round the garden, had festoons of colored lamps that at a distance looked like large brilliant stars seen thro' the branches, and placed all round are marble busts, beautiful little figures of Diana, Cupid, Venus, by the glimmering of the lamps, which are partly concealed by the foliage, give you an idea of enchantment.   Here we strolled among the trees and every moment meet some walking from the thick shade unexpectedly, and come upon us before we heard a sound, 'twas delightful! We passed a box that Miss Watts was in ; she called us, and we went in and had a charming, refreshing glass of ice cream, which has chilled me ever since. They have a fine orchestra and have concerts here sometimes. I can conceive of nothing more charming than this must be.

We went on to the Battery : this is a large promenade by the shore of the North River ; very extensive rows and clusters of trees in every part, and a large walk along the shore, almost over the water, gives you such a fresh, delightful air, that every evening in summer it is crowded with company. Here too they have music playing on the water in boats of a moonlight night. Last night we went to a garden[1] a little out of town,

---

[1] *Mt. Vernon* Gardens, afterwards called Contois's Gardens, were on the northwest corner of Broadway and Leonard Street.

Mount Vernon garden, — this too is surrounded by
boxes of the same kind, with a walk on top of them.
You can see the gardens all below; but 'tis a *summer
playhouse* — pit and boxes, stage and all, but open on
top; from this there are doors opening into the garden,
which is similar to Columbia Garden, lamps among the
trees, large mineral fountain, delightful swings, two at
a time, — I was in raptures as you may imagine, and if
I had not grown sober before I came to this wonderful
place 'twould have turned my head. But I have filled
my letter and not told you half — of the Park — the
public buildings, — I have so much to tell you, and of
those that have called on me — I have no room to say
half. Yesterday Mrs. Henderson came again to see me
and brought two of my Aunt King's most intimate
friends to introduce — Mrs. Delafield [1] and Miss Lucy
Bull. Mr. and Mrs. Delafield are Uncle and Aunt's
very intimate friends, she is called the most elegant
woman in New York. I was delighted with her and
very much gratified at Mrs. Henderson's attention in
coming again on purpose to introduce them, they were
so attentive, so polite, and Mrs. Delafield said so many
things of Aunt King, how delighted they would be to

---

[1] Mrs. Delafield was a Miss Hallett. She married, December 11th,
1784, Mr. John Delafield, an Englishman, who had arrived in New York
in 1783. They had twelve children. Among them were Major Joseph
Delafield, who married Miss Livingston ; Mr. Rufus Delafield married
Miss Bard ; Dr. Edward Delafield married Miss Floyd ; Henry Delafield
married Miss Munson.

find me settled near them, how much I should love them and everything of the kind, that was very gratifying to me. Miss Denning has been to see me 3 or 4 times; several invitations to tea, but we declined as our family friends were visiting us this week. This morning we go to make calls. I have got a list of names that most frightens me. All our brothers and sisters say — " Why, Eliza does not seem at all like a stranger to us," — indeed I feel as easy and happy among them as possible, which astonishes me, as I have been so unaccustomed to Quakers, but their manners are so affectionate and soft, you cannot help it. Mrs. King (sister) is a beauty — She would be very handsome in a different dress; she looks so much like Alicia Wyer, you would love her, — just such full sweet blue eyes, charming complexion and sweet expression, and her little quaker cap gives her such an innocent, simple appearance, I imagine Alicia with a quaker dress — and you will see her exactly. Adieu. I am expecting to hear from you every day. Mr. Bowne is out, would send a great deal of love if he were here. Kiss dear little Mary and all the children. I never go by a toy shop, or confectionery, without longing to have them here. Love to all. Our best love to my Father and Mother, Horatio, Isabella and all. I mean to write as soon as I am settled a little. Adieu.

Miss Southgate.

New York, June 18, 1803.

I am just going to set off for Long Island and therefore promise but a short letter. I have a mantua maker
here making you a gown which I hope to have finished
to send by Mrs. Rodman. The fashions are *remarkably
plain*, sleeves much longer than ours, and half handkerchiefs are universally worn. At Mrs. Henderson's
party there was but one lady except myself without a
handkerchief, — dressed as plain as possible, the most
fashionable women the plainest. I have got you a
pretty India spotted muslin, — 'tis fashionable here.
My husband sends a great deal of love, says we shall
be travelling about all Summer, settle down soberly in
October, and depend on seeing you as soon as we are
at housekeeping. Sister Caroline has made Sister Boyd
a tasty quaker cap, which I shall send with the gown.
How could you mistake what I said of Caroline so
much? Far from being *"stiff and rigid,"* she is most
affectionate, attentive and obliging, — nothing was more
foreign to my thoughts, and you must have taken your
idea from what I said of her dress, which, you may
depend upon it, with quakers is no criterion to judge
by. I never was more disappointed in my life — to find
such a stiff, forbidding external covered so much affability and sweetness.

You must give my love to Miranda. I wish I had
time to write to her, Horatio, my Mother and all, but I
expect the carriage every moment. Tell Horatio he

must write to me. At present my letters to you must answer for all, till I am more settled. Mrs. Codman has promised to call at our house and tell you all about me. Malbone[1] has just finished my picture; I have done sitting; he was not willing I should see it, as 'tis unfinished. When you return 'twill be done, then I'll tell you whether 'tis like. I have told you in a former letter we shall go to Bethlehem, Philadelphia, and perhaps to the Springs. My trunk arrived safe. I shall send a little ring to Cousin Mary Porter; 'tis not the kind I wanted, but I had not time to have one made to send by Mrs. C. Is mine with sister Mary's hair done? Send it to her by the first opportunity. Adieu. Best love to all friends, and all the children. Tell mamma I mean to write her as soon as I have leisure, that I am very, *very* happy, that Uncle Rufus has *not* arrived, tho' every day expected, and that I look to the time when we shall see her and my Father in New York. Mr. Bowne and myself both will be delighted. Give my best love to Lucia,[2] Zilpah and John, and ask the latter

[1] *Malbone*, a celebrated miniature painter. He was born at Newport, Rhode Island, and when very young showed great taste for painting. He travelled about the then known portions of the United States, painting portraits of people in Charleston, Boston, Philadelphia, New York, etc., many of which are now in existence. His price for painting a head was $50. He died of consumption in Savannah, May 7, 1807, in the thirty-second year of his age.

[2] Lucia, Zilpah, and John were the children of Genl. Peleg Wadsworth. Zilpah afterwards married Stephen Longfellow, and was the mother of Henry Wadsworth Longfellow. Genl. Wadsworth lived at Hiram, on the Saco River.

ZILPAH WADSWORTH

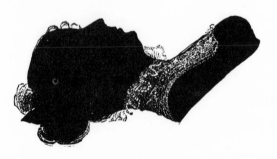

LUCIA WADSWORTH

if he has discovered on whom my *mantle rested.* Tell Zilpah we pass her friend Mrs. Bogert's house every day, and never without thinking of her. The City air has not stolen my *country bloom* yet, for every one says — " I need not ask you how you do, Mrs. Bowne, you look in such fine health." Dr. Moore [1] would not inoculate me for the Small Pox, after examining my arm, as he was sure from what I told him I had had the Kine Pox well, and he would insure me against the Small Pox. But Mr. Bowne seems to wish I should be inoculated, tho' I care nothing about it now. Adieu. My best love to Aunt Porter and Nancy, Mary Porter and all the other friends. We are going to *Flushing* to see our cousins before we return ; you know how Mary laughed about the name. Yesterday we were at Belvidere, the most beautiful place, the finest view in the world, the greatest variety. I never shall have done. Kiss dear little Mary ; I think of her every time I see a sweet little sight. Your affectionate sister

ELIZA S. BOWNE.

P. S. Remember and put an S in my name to distinguish ; there are 2 or 3 Eliza Bownes in the family.

[1] Dr. William Moore was a celebrated physician of New York. He married Miss Sarah Fish and had by her a numerous family. Among them being Nathaniel Moore, President of Columbia College, and Dr. Samuel Moore, also a favorite physician.

New York, June 30, 1803.

Uncle Rufus [1] has just landed.   The Hussas have
ceased, the populace retired, and I hasten to give you
the earliest information.   Several thousand people were
on the wharf when he landed, my Husband among
the number.   As he stept from the vessel they gave 3
cheers and escorted him up into Broadway to a Mr.
Nicholas Lowe's [2] (his friend) ; then three more cheers as
he entered the door.   He stood at the door, bowed, and
they dispersed — all but a dozen particular friends, who
accompanied him into the house, and Mr. Bowne with
them.   Was introduced by Mr. Watson,[3] and immediately after Mr. Henderson [4] said, " A niece of yours, Mr.
King ; was lately married in New York to Mr. Bowne."
My Uncle immediately came up to him, shook hands a
second time, and said, "*Miss Southgate*, I presume." —
He staid but a few moments ; the acclamations of the
people had rather embarrassed him (uncle).   Aunt King
had not landed.   This evening we are going to see them.
Imagine me entering, presented by Mrs. Henderson,
Miss Bull, or Mrs. Delafield, — all her intimate friends ;

[1] He was returning from his mission in London, where he had been
Minister to the Court of St. James from the United States.

[2] Nicholas Low, a merchant in New York.   Among his descendants
are Mrs. Eugene Schuyler and the wife of M. Waddington, at present
ambassador to the Court of St. James from France.

[3] Mr. Watson was at this time a widower with one son, James Watson.
This son became a great beau in New York society, but died unmarried
and insane.

[4] William Henderson, who had married Sarah Denning.

think what a mixture of sensations! I'll tell you all about it. I returned from Long Island this morning: delightful sail, beautiful country, and pleasant visit. Malbone has finished my picture, but is unwilling we should have it as the likeness is not striking, — he says not handsome enough — so says Mr. B. But I think 'tis in some things much flattered. It looks too serious, pensive, soft, — that's not *my* style at all. But perhaps 'twill look different; 'twas not quite finished when I saw it; however, he insists on taking it again as soon as he returns from the Southward, and told Mr. Bowne, if he *must* have one he might keep this till he returned and he would try again. Uncle Rufus brings news that *war* has actually taken place, hostilities commenced. The King[1] on the 14th sent a message to Parliament that he was determined to use every effort to repress the overbearing power of France, and hoped for their united assistance and exertions. — So much for *Father.* — The whole City seems alive, nothing else talked of but the arrival of Mr. King and the news of War. Adieu. I'll write again soon. Best love to all the family.

We are in expectation of great entertainment on fourth of July — *Independent* day! as they laugh at us Yankees for calling it, — the gardens, the Battery, and every thing to be illuminated, fire-works, music, etc., etc. Col. Boyd called to see me; and Mr. Grelett, whom I was introduced to in Boston, brought the handsome Miss Pemberton, whom you have heard Col. B. speak of — to

[1] George III of England.

call on me ; she's from Philadelphia. I was out. I hope none of my acquaintance will come to New York, pass thro', or any thing, without finding me out.   I just begin to make memorandums of tables and chairs, spoons and beds, and everything else ; most turns my brain, so many things to think of ; but I am well and happy, and 'tis a pleasant task.   Adieu.

Yours affectionately,   ELIZA S. BOWNE.

10 o'clock, evening.

Just returned from Uncle Rufus'. Mr. B. introduced me to Uncle ; he took my hand, introduced us to his wife, and they both seemed much pleased to see us. Uncle is so easy and graceful and pleasing, I was delighted with him. Looks very like *Mr. Parker* instead of *Mr. Davis* ; enquired particularly after the family ; was surprised at my being here, — said everything that was pleasant, hoped we should be very sociable, etc., etc. ; and after a pleasant half-hour we returned home. I broke the seal of my letter to tell you ; 'tis late, I can't be particular.   E. S. B.

Miss Southgate, Portland.

New York, July 4, 1803.

Dear Mother :

I have written generally to Octavia, but as I meant my letters for the family, 'tis not much matter to whom they were directed. I wrote you of Uncle Rufus' arrival and our calling on them the evening after. Sunday they called on us with Mr. and Mrs. Lowe, their friends, with whom they are staying till their own house is ready. They both kissed me very affectionately, said everything that pleased me, and were very solicitous that we might get houses near each other in the winter, that we might be sociable neighbors. Uncle Rufus says I remind him of Martha very much ; he inquired particularly after all the family, and asked if I did not expect you would come on to see me, and both appeared much pleased when I assured them I depended on seeing you here. Aunt King told Mr. Bowne he must bring me to see them *very often,* and look upon her as a *Mother.*

July 8.

My letter will be an old date before I finish it. You must have perceived, my Dear Mother, from my letters, that I am much pleased with New York. I was never in a place that I should prefer as a situation for life, and nothing but the distance from my friends can render it other than delightful. We have thus far spent the summer delightfully : we have been no very long journeys, but been on a number of little excursions of 20 or 40 miles to see whatever is pleasant in the neighborhood. Mr. Bowne's friends, tho' all very plain, are very amiable and affectionate, and I receive every attention from them I wish. I have a great many people call on me, and shall have it in my power to select just such a circle of acquaintance as suits my taste, — few people whose prospects of happiness exceed mine, which I often think of with grateful sensations. Mr. Bowne's situation in life is equal to my most sanguine expectations, and it is a peculiar gratification to me to find him so much and so universally esteemed and respected. This would be ridiculous from me to any but my Mother, but I know it must be pleasing to you to know that I realize all the happiness you can wish me. I have not a wish that is not gratified as soon as 'tis known. We intend going to Bethlehem, Philadelphia, and a watering place, similar to the Springs, about 30 miles beyond Philadelphia; shall probably set out the latter part of this month. At present we have done nothing toward housekeeping, and Mr. Bowne won't let me do the least thing towards it, lest I get my mind engaged and not enjoy the pleasure of our journeys. — 'Tis very different here from most any place, for there is no article but you can find ready made to your taste, excepting table linen, bedding, etc., etc. One poor bed quilt is all I have towards housekeeping, and been married two months almost. I am sadly off, to be sure. We have not yet found a house that suits us. Mr. Bowne don't like any of his own, and wishes to hire one for the present until he can *build*, which he intends doing next season; which I am very glad of, as I never liked living in a hired house and changing about so often. Uncle and Aunt King want we should get near them; they have hired a ready furnished house about 2 miles out of the city for the summer, and intend hiring a house in town in the winter. I have been very busy with my mantua-maker, as I am having a dress made to wear to Mrs. Delafield's to dine on Sunday ; they have a most superb country seat on Long Island, opposite Hell-Gate; — he is Uncle Rufus' most intimate friend and a very intimate one of Mr. Bowne's. We shall probably meet them there ; I have not seen them to ask. My picture is done, but I am disappointed in it. Malbone says he has not done me justice, so says Mr. Bowne ; but I think, tho' the features are striking, he has not caught the expression, particularly of the eyes, which are excessively *pensive:* would do for Sterne's Maria. The mouth laughs a little and they all say is good, — all the lower part of the face ; but the eyes not the thing. He wants me to sit again, so does Mr. Bowne. Malbone thinks he could do much better in another position. I get so tired, I am quite reluctant about sitting again. However, we intend showing it to some of our friends before we determine. How do all our friends at Saco and Topsham do ? I often think of them, and Mr. Bowne and myself are talking of coming to see you next summer very seriously. How comes on the new house ? We are to come as soon as ever that is finished. If you choose to send so far, I will purchase any kind of furniture you wish, perhaps cheaper and better than you can get elsewhere. Adieu. Remember me to all the children. Dear little Mary, — I can't help crying sometimes, with all my pleasures and amusements ; 'tis impossible to be at once reconciled to quitting all one's friends. I thought a great deal of the children. I never thought I loved them so much; I

never pass a toy-shop or confectionery without wishing
them here.   How does Horatio succeed in business, as
well as he expected?   How comes on Father's turnpike
and diking?   Tell him I yesterday met a woman full
broke out with the small-pox; I was within a yard of her
before I perceived it; the first sensation was terror, and
I ran several paces before I recollected myself.   As
soon as I arrived in town Doctor Moore examined my
arm, enquired the particulars, and refused to inoculate
me again; that he would venture to insure me from the
small-pox; that he had inoculated hundreds and never
had one take the small-pox after the kine-pox.   Adieu.

Your affectionate daughter

ELIZA S. BOWNE.

P. S.   All the family desire to be remembered particularly.   Mr. B. is out to dine.

Mrs. Southgate, Scarborough, District of Maine.

New York, July 14.

Friend Greene from Portland is here and will dine
with us to-day; a fine opportunity for me to write to my
friends.   I have quite a packet of newspapers which I
shall send by him to amuse you; they contain all the
public amusements and shows in celebration of 4th July.
The Procession passed our house and was very elegant.
In the evening we were at Davis Hall Gardens; the
entertainment there you will see by the papers; 'twas
supposed there were 4,000 people there; tickets half a

SUNSWICK—THE DELAFIELD HOUSE
Hell Gate, Long Island

dollar; and 'tis said he made very little money, so you
may think what the entertainment was. Indeed there is
every day something new and amusing to me. Whenever we have nothing particular in view, in the cool of
the evening we walk down to the Battery, go into the
garden, sit half an hour, eat ice-cream, drink lemonade,
hear fine music, see a variety of people, and return home
happy and refreshed. Sunday we dined at Mr. Delafield's near Hell Gate, Long Island; the most superb,
magnificent place I ever saw, situated directly on the
East river, the finest view you can imagine. I was delighted with our visit, so much ease, elegance and hospitality. I am very glad you liked your gown. Long
sleeves are very much worn, made like mitts; cross-
wise, only one seam and that in the back of the arm,
and a half drawn sleeve over and a close, very short one
up high, drawn up with a cord. I have just been having one made so. All Mrs. Delafield's daughters, even
to little Caroline, no older than our Mary, had their
frocks made exactly like the gown I sent you, only cut
open in the back, a piece of bone each side and eyelet
holes laced, — long sleeves as I mentioned above; short
sleeves and open behind. I should admire to be in
Portland, now all the Coffin family are there. Give my
best love to Mrs. Coffin and Ellen Foster; the others
will have returned. I am astonished at what you say
about my calling on Mrs. Sumner, and what Mrs.
Coffin said. When I got to Boston I determined to
call nowhere but at Mrs. Sumner's, as my intimacy in

the family was such and I was fearful she might not
hear of my being in town and should not see her; accordingly the day I got in town we went out purposely
to call there, and to prevent any one calling on us (for I
did not wish to see much company) we said we expected
to go out of town immediately. However, there were
a great many called to see me notwithstanding. In
Cap hill we met Mr. Sumner. I introduced Mr. Bowne,
said we were just going to call on Mrs. Sumner, enquired how she did, etc., and Mr. Sumner said they were
just going out to ride, but if I would go immediately
with him I could see her. I was fearful of detaining
them, and thought I should certainly see her, now she
knew I was in town and had set out to call on her; and
Mr. Sumner particularly asked where we were to be
found, — we told him Mrs. Carter's, and parted. From
that time, every time I heard the bell, I supposed 'twas
Mrs. Sumner. We staid 2 days, and neither Mr. nor
Mrs. Sumner called. I felt amazingly hurt, as so many
ladies I was very little acquainted with called on me
immediately. Late in the evening before we left town,
Tom Coffin called in, appeared rather formal, never
mentioned Mrs. Sumner or any reason why they did
not call, nor any apology. As I could no way account
for such mysterious conduct, it greatly mortified me.
This is the true statement, which you may mention to
Mrs. Coffin, and then ask her who has a right to feel
offended. The great dinner given in honor of Uncle
Rufus I have not yet mentioned; 'twas very superb, and

200 of the most respectable citizens of New York attended. Mr. Bowne says, tho' he has been at many entertainments given in honor of particular persons, yet he never saw one that was so complimentary, and never a person conduct himself on such an occasion with such ease, elegance, and dignity in his life. He returned quite in raptures, — such insinuating manners — such ease in receiving those presented and introduced, — he is a most amazing favorite here. Democrats and Federalists and all parties attended. French Consul on his right — English Consul on his left. When Mr. Bowne went up, he held out his hand with all the ease of an old friend, without even bowing, and said, " How ! is it Bowne ? How 's your wife ? " — so familiar. I went to see the tables : very novel and elegant — there was one the whole length of the Hall and 4 branches from it ; there was an enclosure about 2 feet wide, filled with earth, and railed in with a little white fence, and little gates every yard or two ran thro' the centre of all the tables, and on each side were the plates and dishes. In this enclosure there were lakes, and swans swimming, little mounds covered with goats among little trees, — some places flocks of sheep, some cows laying down, beautiful little arches and arbors covered with green, — figures of Apollo, Ceres, Flora, little white pyramids with earth and sprigs of myrtle, orange, lemon, flowers in imitation of hothouse plants, — nothing could have a more beautiful effect in the hot weather ; those opposite to you were divided, their plates quite hidden. Adieu ;

some ladies have just called. We are going about 20
miles to enjoy the sea, Rockaway, a place of fashionable
resort; 'tis intensely hot, exceeded only by Ballston
Springs. We don't go to Bethlehem till the last of the
month. Mr. Bowne's business detains him in the City
only one or two days in a week perhaps, yet prevents a
long journey just now. We ride out every day or two,
go into the baths whenever we please, they have very
fine public ones. Adieu. The ladies will think I am
Yankee. Love to all.   ELIZA S. BOWNE.

Sally Weeks remember me to — and all other friends ;
Betsey Tappan — tell her Mr. Bowne often speaks of
that sweet little Miss Tappan. How comes on Father's
house, Octavia ? We both depend on its being finished
next season. We think very seriously of coming next
summer. Mr. Bowne wants to go almost as much as
myself.

Love to Sister, hope she is well again. Uncle Rufus
told me Mr. Boyd had been very sick, but I did not
mention it, lest it might alarm sister. Adieu. Love to
Zilpah and Lucia. Tell Zilpah Mrs. Bogert came to see
me last week and is in hopes she will come on with her
father. Remember me affectionately to all Mrs. Davis'
family. I sometimes treat myself with telling my Husband all about our charming frolics. Does not Mr.
Davis talk anything of coming to New York ? Louise
is quite a belle I suppose.

Miss Southgate.

New York, July 23, 1803.

I have sent a few sugar toys to the children, which
you must divide, — the cradle for Mary, the basket for
Arixene, etc., etc., — pair shoes apiece, two little dogs I
put up in the music — one looks like Sancho ; a little
frock I send as a pattern for Miranda, Arixene, and
Mary, long or short sleeves as you please, whalebone in
the back, laced. I have sent another box of things to
Isabella's children : the paper box I mean for them ; two
little fans for Arixene and Mary, with their names on
them, you'll find in the bottom of the box. The two songs
I sent you are all I could find that struck me ; for the
"Death of Allen," I never heard it, and bought it be-
cause it was a composition of Floyd's ; "The Wounded
Hussar" I admired and knew you could not get it set
for the Piano, — I don't know but 'tis different from
Miss Sandford's. I write in great haste — we are going
to dine at Uncle Rufus' out of town ; 'tis past eleven.
They have a delightful place on the North River ; took
tea there last week. Mr. Bowne joins me in love to
Father and Mother and all. How comes on the house,
Octavia ? — we want to come very much next Summer.
Adieu.

Yours,   E. S. B.

P. S. I have some fine peaches and apricots on the
table before me ; Mr. Bowne brings me a pocketful of
fruit every time he comes home. I have ate as many

as I want to, and have been thinking how much I would give to get them to you, but this early fruit won't keep at all.   I was at the theatre night before last — at Mount Vernon Garden; Hodgkinson is a fine fellow. We commence our Southern journey in about 10 days. Oh, I am sorry — Mr. Bowne just came to tell me the vessel has sailed — well, I must wait for another.   Love to Mary Porter, and give her the ring I enclose of my hair; tell her I long to see her, and ask if she means to be *Mary Porter* when I next come to the Eastward. Love to all friends.

Miss Octavia Southgate.   ELIZA S. BOWNE.

Bethlehem, August 9, 1803.

I intended writing before I left New York, but was so much engaged in preparing for our journey, I had no time.   My great wish to see this famous Bethlehem [1] is at length gratified.   You can scarcely imagine any

---

[1] Bethlehem.   This is a place originally settled by a religious sect called Moravians.   They were famous for their schools, — one for boys kept by the Brothers, and a girls' school kept by the Sisters.   Young ladies were sent to Bethlehem from New York, Philadelphia, and distant parts of the country, to receive their education at this place.   In a letter from John Adams to his daughter, dated Monday, Feb. 10th, 1823, he speaks of it: " I have seen a remarkable institution for the education of young ladies at Bethlehem.   About 120 of them live under the same roof. They sleep all together in the same garret.   I saw 120 beds in two long rows in the same room.   The beds and bedclothes were all of excellent quality and extraordinary neat.   How should you like to live in such a nunnery ? "

thing more novel and delightful than every thing about here, so entirely different from any place in New England. Indeed, in travelling thro' the State of Pennsylvania, the cultivation, buildings, and every thing are entirely different from ours, — highly cultivated country, looks like excellent farmers. Barns twice as large as the houses, all built of *stone ;* no white painted houses, as in New England. We crossed the famous Delaware at Easton. It separates New Jersey and Pennsylvania. We saw some beautiful little towns in New Jersey likewise, but in Pennsylvania the villages look so many clusters of *jails*, and the public buildings like the Bastile, or, to come nearer home, like the New York State prison, — all of *stone*, so strong, heavy, and gloomy, I could not bear them ; the inhabitants most all Dutch, and such *jargon* as you hear in every entry or corner makes you fancy yourself in a foreign country. These Bethlehemites are all Germans, and retain many of the peculiarities of their country — such as their great fondness for music. It is delightful : there is scarcely a house in the place without a Piano-forte ; the Post Master has an elegant grand Piano. The Barber plays on almost every kind of music. Sunday afternoon we went to the Young Men's house to hear some sacred music. We went into a hall, which was hung round with Musical Instruments, and about 20 musicians of the Brethren were playing in concert, — an organ, 2 bass viols, 4 violins, two flutes, two French horns, two clarionets, bassoon, and an Instrument I never heard before, made up the Band; they all seemed animated and interested. It was delightful to see these men, who are accustomed to laborious employments, all kinds of mechanics, and so perfect in so refined an art as music. One man appeared to take the lead and played on several different instruments, and to my great astonishment I saw the famous musician enter the breakfast room this morning with the razor-box in his hand to shave some of the gentlemen. Judge of my surprise; and some one mentioned he had just been fixing a watch down-stairs. Yesterday, Daddy Thomas (who is a head one, and who comes to the tavern every few hours to see if there are any strangers who wish to visit the buildings) conducted us all round. We went to the Schools, — first was merely a *sewing school*, little children, and a pretty single sister about 30, with her white skirt, white, short, tight waistcoat, nice handkerchief pinned outside, a muslin apron and a close cambric cap, of the most singular form you can imagine. I can't describe it; the hair is all put out of sight, turned back before, and no border to the cap, very unbecoming but very singular, tied under the chin with a pink ribbon, — blue for the married, white for the widows. Here was a Piano-forte, and another sister teaching a little girl music. We went thro' all the different schoolrooms — some misses of 16, — their teachers were very agreeable and easy, and in every room was a Piano. I never saw any embroidery so beautiful; Muslin they don't work. Make artificial flowers very handsome, paper baskets, etc. At the single Sisters' house we were conducted round by a fine lady-like woman, who answered our questions with great intelligence and affability. I think there were 130 in this house; their apartments were perfectly neat, — the Dormitory or sleeping-room is a large room in the upper part of the building, with "Dormont" opposite the whole length. A lamp suspended in the middle of the ceiling, which is kept lighted all night; and there were 40 beds, in rows, only one person in each, — they were of a singular shape, high and covered, and struck me like people laid out — dreadful! the lamp and altogether seemed more like a nunnery than any thing I had seen. One sister walks these sleeping-rooms once an hour thro' the night. We went to a room where they keep their work for sale, — pocket-books, pin balls, Toilette cushions, baskets, artificial flowers, etc., etc. We bought a box full of things, and left them much pleased with the neatness and order which appeared thro'out. The situation of the place is delightful. The walks on the banks of the Lehigh and the mountains surrounding — 'tis really beautiful. The widows' house and young men's is similar to the one described; there were many children at the school, from Georgia, Montreal, and many other places as far. There are some genteel people from Georgia at the tavern where we are, and Philadelphia. We intended leaving here for Philadelphia to-day, but it rains. We shall spend a few days there and go to Long Branch. If the alarm of the fever [1]

---

[1] The yellow fever having broken out in New York, the city was deserted by all who could leave it. Even the business was transacted in the

continues in New York we shall not return there again, but go in the neighborhood.   Send in for a trunk, which I packed up for the purpose, in case I feared going in the City — and set off for the Springs or somewhere else.   'Tis very uncertain when we go to housekeeping ; the alarm of the Fever hurried us out of town without any arrangement towards it, and may, if it continues, keep us out till middle of Autumn.   But at any rate you must spend the winter with us, we both depend on it.   You can certainly find some opportunity.   Give my best love to all friends, and expect to hear from me frequently while I am rambling about.   My husband is so fond of roving, I don't know but he'll spoil me.   We

neighboring village of Greenwich, which is now incorporated in the city itself and its boundaries lost in the surrounding streets.   The following advertisements have been copied from the " Evening Post," Thursday, Aug. 25, 1803, as being of interest, as the advertisers were not only well-known New Yorkers, but personal friends of Mrs. Bowne : —

Woolsey & Rogers' Counting House is removed to No. 28 Courtlandt Street.

REMOVAL.   William Codman has removed his Counting House to the N. E. corner room in the 2nd Story of the City Hotel, Broadway.

John G. Bogart, Attorney at law & Notary Public, has Removed his office to the House of Judge Livingston, No. 37 Broadway, near the Custom House.

John Murray & Sons have removed their Counting House to Mr. Murray's country seat on the Harlem Road, 3 1-2 miles from town.

[This was at Murray Hill, about the corner of 37th Street and Fifth Avenue.]

The Editor being obliged to be absent from town a few days, the discussions respecting *yellow fever* will, of course, be suspended for a little time.

both enjoy travelling very much, and surely it is never so delightful as in company with those we love. Only think, 'tis just *a year* to-day since we first saw each other, and here we are, Married, happy, and enjoying ourselves in Bethlehem. Memorable day! Horatio's and Frederick's *birthday*, too ; mine will soon be here. I long to see you all more than you can imagine ; hope to, next summer, and *depend* on your spending the winter with us. Love to Miranda, when you write, and tell her I mean to write myself. Mr. B—— often talks of her. Is Mr. Boyd[1] *arrived?* I want much to hear. Love to Sister[2] and the children. Adieu.

> Affectionately,
>
> ELIZA S. BOWNE.

Mrs. Southgate, Scarborough.

Ballston Springs, Sept. 4, 1803.

Once more do I write you from the *Springs*, where I enjoyed so many delightful moments last year. We recall so many charming things to our recollection by this visit to the Springs that 'tis of all places the most pleasant for us to visit. A description of the place, amusements, etc. I gave you last year ; they are the same now. We arrived yesterday morning, found the place much crowded, and were fearful of not getting good accommo-

---

[1] Mr. Boyd, Mrs. Bowne's brother-in-law, had been in England for some months and was now expected to return to his home.

[2] Mrs. Boyd, Isabella Southgate.

dations, but in that respect were agreeably disappointed. They dance much as usual; a fine ball to-morrow evening. I wish you were here to help us dance, — a great many New Yorkers have taken refuge here from the fever. I was quite sorry when I found Mr. Derby had been here and gone again. Tell Louise the *Bussey* family from Boston are here, and Miss Putnam appears as much delighted with the *picturesque steeps* of Ballston as she was with those of *Freeport*, and with about as much reason. We have an abundance of queer, smart people here. Last night at tea I found myself seated alongside *Beau Dawson*,[1] " *Nancy Dawson*," — our envoy to France — you remember! Gen. Smith of Baltimore and family, who it was said would succeed Uncle Rufus; Mr. Harper and wife — the fine speaker in Congress; *Herssa Madame* Somebody — French lady; and a nobleman from nobody knows where, and a parcel of strange people, making a variety that I like once in a while. But, let me see, I have hurried you along to the Springs from Long Branch in a much easier manner than I got here myself. Oh the tremendous Highlands![2] I thought to my soul I should never hold out

[1] Beau Dawson, Mr. J. Dawson of Virginia. He had been sent out by President Jefferson in April, 1801, as bearer of the Treaty or Convention between France and the United States as ratified by the latter. The ship in which he sailed was wrecked and the Treaty lost, although the envoy was saved. Another treaty was drawn up and dispatched as soon as possible, but there was great annoyance at the delay.

[2] Highlands. The hills about West Point on the Hudson are so called. The road from Peekskill to Garrison's over the hill called

to get over them — such roads! But I lived over it,
tho' it made me sick fairly, with fatigue. I went to see
Maria Denning, whose father's country seat, Beverly, is
in the midst of the Highlands — on the North River,
directly opposite *West Point.* It does not look much
like Louisa's picture; 'twould make one of the most sublime and beautiful pictures imaginable if the objects
were selected with judgment. It rises with sublime
and picturesque grandeur directly from the North River.
Who would have thought of taking a view of it without
water? — that is the greatest beauty when united with
the others. We got to Mr. Denning's Saturday night,
— left the neighborhood of New York, Thursday, —
where we staid only one night, dined at Uncle's, drank
tea at Sister Murray's, and set off that evening for the
Springs. The romantic and beautiful scenery on the
North River as we rode up was most charming to me.
I admire the wild diversity of nature — here we had it
in perfection. I am sure the *Hudson* wants nothing but
a Poet to celebrate it. The Thames and the Tiber have
been sung by Homers and Popes, but I don't believe
there can be a greater variety, more sublimity or more
beauty, than are to be found on the banks of the Hudson. The Delaware did not strike me at all — I crossed
it several times. We were in hopes Uncle and Aunt
would come here with us, but Uncle said he must go

" Anthony's Nose " is particularly steep and stony. The Beverly Farm,
which was owned by Mr. William Denning, lay in the midst of these hills.
The house is still standing and is almost unaltered.

East if anywhere, but he wanted to be at rest a few months, now he was settled. Mrs. Codman told me she saw you all; we called a moment to see her. Mrs. Sumner has a son too. Poor Mrs. Davis, how much sickness she has! On our return from Long Branch we went to *Passaic Falls* with a Baltimore family; had a charming little jaunt about 20 miles from New York. The falls — the rocks — the whole scenery partakes more of the sublime — almost terrific — than Glens Falls, but not so beautiful. I am much delighted to hear of Mr. Boyd's arrival; Sister must be very happy. Martha is coming this month; the fever would prevent her coming to New York — I am sorry. Love to Mrs. Coffin. My mother is quite well, Mrs. Codman tells me. Horatio, — Miranda, there's half a dozen wild girls here that would romp to beat her — they are as old as you, but sad romps. We shall stay here about a week, then go to *Lebanon,* where I wish you to direct a letter to me immediately on the receipt of this. I want to hear much, so does Mr. Bowne. He teases me to death to write home that we may hear from you. We depend on your coming on this winter. When we shall be to housekeeping Heaven knows; not even a napkin made, just getting a woman to work, — fixed the things already, when the fever came and we all left the city; so here I am — perfectly unprepared as possible. Adieu. Tell Horatio he has more time than I have, he ought to write me immediately to Lebanon. Lebanon has been quite deserted. Poor Hannah Hamilton's

Mamma died three or four weeks since. The servants at the other house where I kept last summer, wished me joy, — heard Miss Southgate was married to Mr. Bowne. Oh, I have not told you! — saw the tree Major Andre was taken under, and the house where *Arnold* fled from, left his wife and family, — indeed, 'tis the very house Maria lives in. We staid two nights there and promised to go and see them on our return ; charming place, such fruit, 'tis delicious. In the Jerseys, — don't laugh at travellers' stories, — but we really rode over the peaches in the road ; we always kept our case full, William brought us some off the finest trees that hung over the road. Peaches and cream ! — they laugh and say Boston people cry out, "'tis *so* good !" Well, what have I not wrote about ? A little of everything but sentiment ; a dash of that to complete. I am most tired of jaunting ; the mind becomes satiated with variety and description and pants for a little respite of domestic tranquillity. I've done ; I have most forgot how to write sentiment. I have had no time to think since I was married. I don't expect to, this 2 or 3 months, so good-bye.

Miss Octavia Southgate.   ELIZA S. BOWNE.

Lebanon Springs, Sept. 24, 1803.

Your letter, my dear Octavia, has set my head to planning at a great rate. By all means come on with Mr. Cutts ; I am impatient to see you, and I cannot give up the pleasure of having you with me this winter. We shall be at Housekeeping as soon as *possible* after the fever subsides. My husband thinks the plan a very good one. I will write immediately to Aunt King, say that it is uncertain when you arrive, but I have taken the liberty to request Mr. Cutts to leave you with *her* until I demand you. This settled, I proceed. Tell my good Mother not to be afraid. I am as anxious as herself to be settled at home. I am most tired of roving; it begins to grow cold, and I long for a comfortable fireside of my own. What a sweet circle! Octavia, my dear Husband, and myself; when we are alone we'll read, and work like old times. I have spent a most delightful 3 weeks at Ballston and Lebanon. We had a charming company at Ballston, danced a few nights after I wrote you, and I was complimented as Bride again.— Manager bro't me No. 1, — quite time I was out of date.

Lebanon is delightful as ever; we have a small party, ride to see the Shakers, walk, and play at Billiards, work, read, or anything. Tell Mamma, Eunice Loring that was, is here, — she talks a great deal of my Mother and Aunt Porter, wants to see them very much, etc., etc. She is married to a *Mr. Neufville* of Carolina. She is much out of health, talks of going to England in the Spring. She wants to see you, as she says my Mother talk'd of naming you for *her ;* she wishes she had, as she has no children. The box I mentioned was full of sugar things, toys for the children ; two little fans — a little frock for a pattern, and another for Isabella's children, The Children of the Abbey, and Caroline of Lichfield for Mamma, — all in a package together; a letter for Mrs. Coffin and several others. When we left New York Mr. Bowne sent it to a Commission Merchant who does business for several Portland people, and requested him to send it by the first vessel. As you have n't received it, I suppose the fever which broke out immediately after induced him to shut up his store, or perhaps prevented any Portland vessel from coming near the City, and that it now lies in his store. Write me when you set out, and when 'tis probable you will be in New York; direct to New York, probably I shall be near New York in a fortnight. I have but a few moments to write as the stage passes the village at 11. You alarm me about Ellen; pray enquire particularly and tell me all; go to see yourself, and tell her I can imagine no reason why I have never received a line from her since I have been in New York, — nor Lucy Derby, neither Mrs. Coffin. I wrote to, but it seems she did not receive my letter; love to her and all Portland friends. I am expecting every day to hear Martha has arrived. My best love to Sister Boyd and husband. I wrote a line of congratulation to her, but that too is in the package. Adieu. I shall soon see you, and then we will talk what I have not time to write. My husband's best love.

Yours,   Eliza S. Bowne.

New York, October 23, 1803.

I have waited till my patience is quite exhausted. What can have kept you so long in Boston? Mr. Bowne has been at the Stage Office a dozen times, and I have staid at home every forenoon this week to receive your ladyship. I expect to get to housekeeping next week, and am so busy. Mercy on me, what work this housekeeping makes! I am half crazed with sempstresses, waiters, chambermaids, and every thing else — calling to be hired, enquiring characters, such a fuss. I cannot possibly imagine why you are not here. I should have wrote immediately after receiving your letter, but Mr. Bowne was sure you would be here in less than a week. It is possible you may be in Boston to receive this; if not, you will be here or on the way. If you are troubled about a Protector, Mr. Bowne says there has been several *married* gentlemen come on lately, which if you had known of, would have been proper. Perhaps Mr. Davis may hear of some one. At any rate come as soon as possible, for I am very impatient to see you. My best love to Louisa; tell her I should be much delighted to see her in New York this winter, and my Husband frequently says he should like to have Mr. Davis' family near us in New York. I am sure I should with all my heart. Say everything to Mr. and Mrs. Davis for me that bespeaks esteem.

Adieu. Yours always,

Miss Octavia Southgate.   ELIZA S. BOWNE.

Bloomingdale, Nov. 2, 1803.[1]

Mr. Bowne has just bro't me a letter from you in which you mention coming on with Mr. Wood. I am fearful my answer will arrive too late, as your letter has been written nearly a fortnight. At any rate, come on with Mr. Wood if he has not set out. You should not wait for an answer from me — I shall be ready to receive you at any time, at housekeeping or not. We go in town next Monday, every body is moving in; for the last 3 days there has been no death, and for 5 no new cases. If, unfortunately, Mr. Wood should have gone and you not accepted of his protection, come the very next opportunity without consulting me or waiting a moment. I hope to get to housekeeping very soon. We have just returned from Uncle's, where we had been to meet Mr. and Mrs. Paine (Mrs. Doble) from Boston; she is less beautiful than I expected, — charming little daughter. I am more and more delighted with Aunt King, she is so unaffected, easy and ladylike. Margaret and Mr. Duncan married? I expect to hear still stranger things from Portland — now Ellen Foster is married. I *suppose* she is, tho' I have not heard. I am hourly and impatiently expecting to hear from Martha. How unfortunate! What would I give to be nearer! Adieu: 'tis late; come as soon as possible. Give my love to all friends.

Yours affectionately,　　　　　　Eliza S. Bowne.

[1] To Miranda Southgate, or, more likely, to Octavia. (M. K. L.)

New York, Dec. 24, 1803.[1]

My Dear Mother :

Eliza received a letter yesterday from you, where you say you have not received a letter from either of us a long time. I am really surprised at it, as I wrote you very frequently from Boston, and am determined to let you have a letter now every fortnight to let you know what we are doing and whether I am happy. I begin to feel quite at home and certainly never was happier in my life. It is true I sometimes sigh for home, but it is generally when I am in a crowd that I am most there in imagination. But when I am *here* and none but our own family, I have not a single wish ungratified. I am much more pleased with New York on every account than with Boston. As a City it is much superior, the situation is every way as delightful as possible. The inhabitants to me are *much more* pleasing, more ease, more sociability and elegance, yet not so ostentatious, — they dress with remarkable simplicity ; and I think I could spend the winter here and not expend half the money that I must unavoidably do in Boston. There every one dresses, and a person would look singular not to conform ; but here there is such a variety, and the most genteel people dress so plain that one never appears singular. To-morrow is Christmas and we dine at Uncle's ; he is a charming man, looks amazingly like you, so much so that I admire to look at him. She is a very

[1] From Octavia Southgate to Mrs. Southgate.

affable, pleasing woman, and they both appear to be fond of Eliza. We were at a concert last evening; the most delightful music I ever heard. We wished for Horatio all the evening. There is not much gaiety, they tell me, till after the holydays, that is Christmas and New Year. We have been into no parties yet, but have made many sociable visits, which I very much admire. I am very much pleased with all the *friends* we have visited. Old Mrs. Bowne is a fine, motherly old lady; she treats Eliza with as much affection as an own mother, — they all appear to be very glad to see me, and I really feel sometimes as though I was at home; how I long to see you all! How is Arixene and Mary? How I want to see them! How is Papa this winter? Ah! if you were all here! But next spring we shall all be with you. I am afraid you are solitary — if you are, do, my Dear Mother, tell me, find any opportunity, and I'll be with you as soon as you say, — depend on it, I shall never get so attached either to the inhabitants or the gaieties of New York, as to feel reluctant to return home; even in my happiest hours I think of the time with extreme pleasure. This family is the only thing that would root me to the spot, and there is a charm in that which nothing but home can equal. I have promised Eliza a page for you, so I suppose I must close. Give my best love to Father and the children, and believe me your affectionate child,

OCTAVIA SOUTHGATE.

Octavia has reserved me a page in her letter which I

hasten to improve. I thank you, my Dear Mother, for yours, and beg you will often write me, now Octavia is with me and cannot tell me about home. I am at length settled at housekeeping very pleasantly, and do not find it such a tremendous undertaking. I have been fortunate in servants, which makes it much less troublesome; the house we have taken does not altogether please us, but at any time but May 'tis extremely difficult to get a house. In the Spring we shall be able to suit ourselves. Mr. Bowne wishes to build and is trying to find a lot that suits him, — if so, we shall build the next season. Almost everybody in New York hire houses, but I think it much pleasanter living in one's own. I am more and more pleased with New York, there is more ease and sociability than I expected. I admire Uncle and Aunt more and more every day, and Mr. Bowne thinks there never was Uncle's equal, — such a character as he had often imagined, though not supposed existed. I believe I shan't go to the next Assembly; Octavia will go with Aunt King. You say Mr. Bowne must write you, and as a subject mention the dividends from the Insurance Office. In the Summer there was no dividend, no profits; the next dividend will be soon. Mr. Codman thinks there will be a tolerable one, — you shall hear as soon as it takes place; we have received nothing as yet. Uncle and Aunt always inquire particularly about you, and desire to be mentioned. Make my best love to all friends, kiss the children and tell them not to forget sister Eliza. I live in the hope

of seeing you next Autumn — Heaven grant I may not
be disappointed! Remember me with my best love to
my Father and all the family. Adieu; write me soon,
and believe me

   Your affectionate   ELIZA S. BOWNE.

Mrs. Robert Southgate.

            New York, March.

Dear Miranda:

I have been talking of writing to you so long that I
think it is quite time I should talk no longer, but act;
but you should not have waited for me to write. You
knew both Mr. Bowne and myself would have been very
glad to have heard from you, — all about your school,
your acquaintance, amusements or anything, and I have
a thousand things to take up my attention that you have
not. Do you return home this Spring? We shall find
you at home when we come. I have got one or two
trifles I want to send you, but can't find an opportunity;
there are so few people from our way come to New
York, that 'tis very difficult to send anything. I hear
a strange story about Isabella Porter: she is a silly little
girl, and when she is older, will think she acted very
foolishly, — one ought to know more of the world before
she decides on a thing of so much importance; she is a
mere baby and has seen nothing of life. Do you often
hear of Caroline, Miranda? I feel anxious lest she
should not conduct with as much discretion as she

ought, as she never knew the blessing of having a kind, indulgent mother to watch over her and guard her from harm.

When I was in Bethlehem last summer, I got some little caps such as the girls at school wear, and such as the sisters of members of the Society wear. I want to find an opportunity to send them to you. Did you ever read a description of Bethlehem? If you never did, you may find one in some of the Boston Magazines. We had a little book called a "Tour to Bethlehem," which if I can find I will send you. It will give you a very correct idea of the place, society and customs. When I was there, there were 83 girls, from 4 to 16, at the school, from almost every part of the United States. They all wear these little caps tied with a pink ribbon, which looks very pretty where you see so many of them together, — they learn music, embroidery, and all the useful branches of education, — likewise to make artificial flowers and many little things of that kind. Do you ever attempt painting? — 'tis a charming accomplishment, and if you have any taste for it, should certainly cultivate it. Write me soon, and tell me when you are going home and of anything else that interests you. Mr. Bowne often talks of you and now desires to be particularly remembered.

Adieu; remember me to any of my friends who enquire, and believe me

Your affectionate sister,   ELIZA S. BOWNE.

Miranda Southgate.

Rockaway, August 24, 1804.

Dear Girls :

I enclose you a piece of Mr. Blovell's poetry on the Miss Broomes' country seat at Bloomingdale ; as you both know him, I think it will amuse you. I expect Eliza and Jane Watts down here in a few days and should be delighted if you could be here at the same time. I wrote to you, Octavia, on Monday last a long letter, — answer it soon and tell me how far you mean to comply with my proposals. I spent several days at Flushing last week ; they all enquired very affectionately for you ; but I don't know but Miranda is your rival — she is a monstrous favorite among some of them. I believe Mary Murray is engaged and all matters settled. I met the Murrays and Mrs. Ogden at Miss Curtis's ; they came up from New York the same day we did from Rockaway, — very fortunate meeting them, for it rendered my visit doubly pleasant. 'Twas the season for peaches, we feasted finely. I shall attend to your memorandums as soon as possible. Give my best love to Horatio and Nabby, if I may be allowed to connect the names, and tell him my plan. Mr. Bowne says I must write another letter to urge it more strongly; it must be so.   Yours ever,

E. S. BOWNE.

[New York, November 9th, 1804 (?).]

I have been in daily expectation of a letter from you ever since my return and none has yet come. I have not heard a word from Isabella, tho' I have been very anxious. The trunks arrived yesterday with an old letter for me enclosed by Horatio in a *blank* cover, not a word to say how all the family did, particularly Isabella. We are still at our Mother's, and shall probably remain a fortnight longer; the house would be ready in a few days, but we think it is too damp at present. Every body expected you back, for the Murrays had told most of our acquaintance you were to return with me. John and Hannah Murray came to see me the day after I arrived. John rattles as usual, talks much of getting married — his old tune, you know: he has completed his thirtieth year now since we have been gone; he says, "I begin to feel the approach of old age." Mr. Newbold called to enquire particularly after your ladyship, and Mr. Rhinelander[1] spent last evening with us; I think he improves fast; he told me a deal of news. Miss Farquar and Mr. Jepson[2] were married last night, Miss Blackwell and Mr. Forbes, and one or two others. Rhinelander says half the girls in town are to be married before Spring. Maria Denning for one; and the

[1] Mr. Newbold and Mr. Philip Rhinelander were well-known New Yorkers. The latter married, December 22, 1814, Miss Mary Colden Hoffman.

[2] Mr. Jephson was an Englishman who had lately arrived in New York.

world says Amelia and James Gillispie will certainly
make a match,— that I was surprised at.   Miss Bunner[1]
and John Duer are married ; Sally Duer is soon to be;
and Fanny is positively engaged to Mr. Smith, whom
you saw several times last winter, of Princeton.   So
you see all the girls are silly enough to give up their
fine dancing days and become old matrons like myself.
Mrs. Kane is in town ; looks older, paler, and thinner.
She has got a charming little girl,[2] fat and good-natured
as possible.   Mrs. Ogden stays out of town all winter.
We are engaged at Mrs. Bogert's this afternoon, but it
storms so violently I believe I shan't go.   She regrets
very much your not coming, and Lucia [Wadsworth] she
would be delighted to have.   Our things arrived yesterday, but are not out of the vessel yet.   At present
there is no gaiety, quite dull ; there will be a revival
soon, I suppose.   Mr. Poinsett has been to see me
several mornings ; he goes on Monday to Carolina.
Miss de Neufville spends the winter in New York with
her Aunt Stowton.   I meant to call on her this morning, but it was stormy.   The few days I was in Boston
I was constantly engaged.   We dined at Sheriff Allen's

---

[1] John Duer married Miss Anne Bunner October 19, 1804, and his
brother, William Duer, soon after married Maria Denning.   Mr. Rhinelander engaged the two Miss Duers to the wrong men.   Fanny married
Beverly Robinson, and Sally married, March 10, 1805, John Witherspoon
Smith, and died July 10, 1887, in the one hundred and first year of her
age.

[2] Mrs. Kane's "charming little girl" became Mrs. James King of Albany, and the mother of many well-known New Yorkers.

with a very large party, — Lady Temple,[1] Mrs. Winthrop and daughters, Mrs. Bowdoin, Mrs. G. Green, Mrs. Stouton and daughter, and many others, — about 30 ; and we were at Mrs. G. Blake's at a tea-party, she enquired particularly after you ; she is a very fine woman I think.   Our journey on was tolerably pleasant. We arrived before Uncle and Aunt.   Eliza Watts told me she had a letter from you after I left home.   Adieu; write me soon and tell me all the news.   Give my best love to Father, Mother, and all the family.   I am very well and grow fat; everybody says I am wonderfully improved.   Write me soon.

Yours ever,
ELIZA S. BOWNE.

New York, July 30, 1804.

I received your letter, my Dearest Mother, three days since, and every moment of my time and attention since has been taken up with our dear Eliza.   I am grieved that you are so low-spirited about her, tho' as you predicted her trouble has again ended, I yet feel confident if we once get her home, that she will gain strength and do well.   Her Physician has been in great hopes that she would get through this time without any

---

[1] Lady Temple was the daughter of Governor Bowdoin, and had married Sir John Temple.   Their daughter, afterwards Mrs. Winthrop, was the mother of the Hon. Robert C. Winthrop.   She was long the reigning belle in Boston.

THE BOWNE HOUSE—FLUSHING

difficulty, indeed the first week we were in the country
she was so finely, that we all felt encouraged about her.
She had been as prudent as possible, and she can't with
any reason reflect upon herself. The last week we
were there she began to droop again, and Mr. Bowne
brought her into town with an intention of carrying her
to Flushing; now we shall set off for home as soon as
she is strong enough to travel. I am astonished at her
spirits, they are as good again as mine, and yet to-day
she is so much better. I feel finely myself.

She has had no pain, but only suffers from weakness.
We shall go in three or four days to Flushing, which is
a fine, bracing air, and stay there a few days till Eliza
is smart enough to travel 10 miles a day. I place full
confidence in this journey; I am sure that the change
of air and scene, and more than all, the prospect of
home, will render it truly beneficial. We are at Mr.
Bowne's mother's, for we have shut our house up. She
is a fine old lady, and Caroline is perfectly amiable and
as attentive as possible. I am very glad we are here
and in the neighborhood of Mrs. Bogert, for she is all
goodness. I grow more and more anxious every hour
to get home. The city is quite deserted, though it
never was more healthy. There are as few deaths as
there were in the winter. There has been two weeks
of *very cool* weather. I go wandering about and see
scarcely a face I know. I used to complain last winter
of our large acquaintance, and having the house full of
company, but now I exclaim out half a dozen times a

day that "I wished I could see some one I knew." There are gentlemen enough, but no ladies. Uncle and Aunt, I suppose, have nearly set out for Scarborough. I wish we were to be there whilst they are with you. You can have no idea how very anxious I am to return. Was I not so much occupied I should be positively *homesick*, but I have no time to *think* but upon one subject. Kiss the dear children for us *all*, for we are equally anxious to see you. Remember me very affectionately to Sister Boyd and to the children. Before I leave here I shall be in need of a little money. I won't seal my letter to-night, but will write you how she is to-morrow.

July 31.

I did not finish my letter this morning because Eliza did not feel as well as usual, but this afternoon she is better. She is in charming spirits and so very well that we are delighted. She gives her best love to you ; says *she* don't feel *at all* obliged to you for your wishes, and is determined not to join with you. The old lady desires to be remembered, and says, — "If thee was here, thee could do no more for thy child than we have." Indeed she is the most tender, affectionate of women. My best love to my Father. We are in the full of seeing you soon. I shall not make it long before I write again.

Yours affectionately,

O. SOUTHGATE.

June 3, 1805.

Dear Octavia :

Mamma arrived safe and well on Wednesday morning to our great joy, after having a pleasant passage from Newport, staying two days in Boston, two in Newport, and one in Providence. We are going to Uncle's to dine to-day, and I can't persuade Miranda to write a line to let you know Mamma had come, — company coming in every minute, and can but just steal a moment to write. Louise is with you, — I am more than half vexed that I am to be disappointed of the charming winter I had promised myself, with you and Louise to spend it with me, so you need not be surprised if I am rather ill-natured at times. The secret is out, and all your friends, beaux I mean, walk the other side of the street when I meet them. Mary Murray called this morning ; seemed rather disappointed at not having a letter. Eliza Watts thanks you for the wedding-cake as well as myself. Give my best love to Louise as well as all my other friends. We go over into Jersey to-morrow, — E. Watts and Susan go with us, — John Wadsworth. I wish you could have been here while Mamma was. Adieu ; write me soon, and expect a longer letter as soon as I can command a little more time.

Your affectionate   E. S. Bowne.

P. S. Remember I don't call this a *letter*, so no lectures on that head.

Jamaica, October 6, 1805.

I am delighted, my Dear Octavia, to hear you are so finely, and the more so as I hear it from *yourself.* I did not so soon expect such fine effects from the new system of living; I am sure all will be well now. A wedding I suppose next, for I conclude from the melancholy pathos with which you say, you shall " neither have the independence of a married woman, nor of a single," that you don't mean to try the half-way being. However, let the man teaze if he will; do not think of being married until your health is perfectly confirmed, — I would not for the world. 'Tis so late in the season, 'tis not possible I can come to see you this fall, even tho' there should be two weddings in November. And so you talk of spending the winter with me, — how you love to tantalize ! — and wish me to give you the pleasure of refusing me. You know I should be delighted to have you, but you know you never mean to visit New York as Miss Southgate again. Somebody would put on a graver face than he did last fall on a like occasion, and as he had *as much influence* then as to counteract my wishes, I won't subject myself to the mortification of another defeat now I know his power to be much greater. However I won't ask, tho' I shall be very happy to have you with me. As for news, you give me more than I can you. We have left Rockaway more than a week ago, still exiled from our home by this dreadful calamity. We are at lodg-

ings in Jamaica, where we shall probably remain until
'tis safe removing to the City.   Uncle and Aunt, — Mr.
and Mrs. Bogert,[1] have gone about 30 miles down the
Island, sporting for *Grouse*, and return to Jamaica until
we can all go in town.   Mr. and Mrs. Rogers (Cruger
that was) have taken a house in Jamaica during the
fever; the next door to this I lodge in.   Mr. and Mrs.
Hayward[2] are with them, but leave here for Charleston
this week.   I am in there half of my time.   We make a
snug little party at *Brag* in the evening frequently, and
work together mornings.   Mr. Bowne goes to Greenwich, where all the business is transacted, on Mondays
and Thursdays, but returns the same night, so I am
but little alone.   As to news — Miss Charlotte Manden
Heard was married last week to a *gentleman* from *De-
marara*, whom nobody knew she was engaged to until
he came a few weeks since and they were married.
John Murray, I believe, is at last really in love, tho'
'tis not yet determined whether the lady smiles or not.
A Miss Rogers from Baltimore, whom he met at the
Springs, — a sweet interesting girl, 'tis said.   Wolsey
Rogers[3] and Harriet Clarke[4] were talked of as a match

[1] Mr. and Mrs. Bogert were intimate friends of Mr. and Mrs. Rufus
King's, and they occupied adjoining places at Jamaica.

[2] Mrs. Heyward was Mr. and Mrs. Rogers' daughter.   She married Mr.
Heyward of South Carolina.   Miss Heyward married Mr. Cutting of New
York, and was the mother of Messrs. William, Heyward, and Brockholst
Cutting.

[3] Wolsey Rogers married, Thursday evening, December 1, 1807, Miss
Susan Bayard.

[4] Harriet Clarke, a daughter of John Innes Clarke of Providence, and
sister of Mrs. Kane.

at the Springs.   Mrs. Kane [1] staid at the Springs till she
was so late she could not venture to ride to Providence
with her Mother, and the fever kept her from New
York, so was obliged to stop at Mrs. Gilbert Living-
stone's [2] — Mr. Kane's sister — at Red Hook, until able
to resume her journey home, which will probably be in
November.   Mrs. Fish [3] has a daughter ; great joy on
the occasion.   Give my love to Cousin Pauline,[4] and
tell her I congratulate her on the birth of her son.
What do Mary [5] and Paulina call their boys — Nathaniel
and Enoch?   I hope not, never keep up such ugly
names.   Mr. B. says you must spend the winter with
us, — he will come under bonds to somebody to return
you safe.   Give my best love to Sister Boyd, Horatio,
and all the family at home.   Has any progress been
made in the new house ?   I am sorry to say I fear not
— 'tis pity, — I had almost said 'tis wrong.   I am half
mortified when I hear of any of my acquaintance visit-

[1] Mrs. Oliver Kane had married, at Providence, R. I., May 22, 1803,
Mr. Oliver Kane, merchant of this city.   Her children were Mrs. King
of Albany, Mrs. William Russel, Mrs. Nicholsen, John, De Lancey, and
Miss Lydia Kane.

[2] Mrs. Gilbert R. Livingston (Martha Kane), a sister of Oliver Kane.
Her children were Mrs. Henry Beekman, Mrs. Codwise, Mrs. Constable,
the Rev. Gilbert R. Livingston, and James Kane Livingston.

[3] Mrs. Fish (Miss Elizabeth Stuyvesant) had married, April 30, 1803,
Colonel Nicholas Fish.   This daughter was Mrs. Daniel le Roy.   The Hon.
Hamilton Fish and Mrs. Richard Morris were also children of Colonel
Fish's.

[4] *Pauline Porter*, daughter of Paulina King and Dr. Aaron Porter of
Portland, had married Edward Beecher.

[5] Mary King Porter, her sister, married Nathaniel Coffin of Saco.

ing Portland, — 'tis true, I declare, — tho' Husband would scold me for saying so. Pappa is an affectionate Father, yet therein he acts not up to his character. I must check my pen — I am too much interested in this subject. Adieu; make my compliments to all acquaintances and write me again soon. Love to Miranda — tell her Mrs. Bogert talks much of her, and remind her from me of Aunt's sleeves ; are they finished ? — if they are, I hope she will send them by Mrs. McKersen. I am working me a beautiful dress, — it will be when 'tis done. By-the-by, any purchases for the coming occasion will be executed with pleasure. Give my best love to (sister I had almost said) Nabby,[1] and tell her I shall feel myself flattered by any commission she will give me either in clothes or furniture ; do away her modesty in this thing, if you think I can be of any service in that way, for I assure you 'twill gratify me. Tell Horatio[1] I am impatient to thank him for giving so pleasant an acquisition to our family, but I could do it more heartily in person in New York, if so I might be indulged. Since you won't be honest and tell the truth, I won't tell you what I'll say to you. Do ask Papa if he could send us 6 or 8 barrels of potatoes, there is like to be a great scarcity in New York ; put them in the hold of the vessel or anywhere. Col. Barclay has sent to Nova Scotia for a vessel load, — a housekeeper —

What a romantic conclusion. Yours, E. B.

---

[1] Horatio Southgate married his first wife, Nabby McLellan, September 29, 1805. Mrs. Bowne is here alluding to her sister Octavia's engagement to William Browne.

New York, Nov. 10, 1805.

Horatio is really married then ; and we not married ; and I suppose the next account your ladyship will be added to the list. How swimmingly you all go on! What a tremendous *marrying* place Portland is. New Yorkers don't marry — sad sett of them. I am half angry to think you are marrying in such an out-of-the-way season, that 'tis impossible any one can come to see you. However, I hope to come early in the summer, if nothing happens to prevent, and spend 3 or 4 months. I shall have so many new relations that 'twill be necessary to come often to keep an account. Robert Murray [1] came home quite delighted with his eastern visit, but disappointed at seeing so little of Miranda. What has been the matter with her, any thing more than a heavy cold? I wish she was here with all my heart. I am quite alone and require a companion more than ever, but I suppose Mamma could not hear of that. I wish Arixene and Mary could have found a good opportunity to come this fall, and we could take them home in the summer, — but I suppose I must be content. We have been in town since the 31st of October, the day your letter was dated ; it has been a long time in coming. I got it only last evening. Mr. Bowne had found out Capt. Libby, and we were preparing to send the sheeting and diaper by him ; he sails the last of the week ; the other things you wish we will send as many as can

1 Robert Murray, Mr. Bowne's nephew.

be procured before the vessel sails, but 'twill be impossible to get any *plate made* to send for several weeks, — we will order it immediately, and as it will not be bulky, there will probably be no difficulty in finding a conveyance. We made a sketch of the articles you wished and of the pieces, which cannot be very incorrect, as I took them all from our own furniture book, and we calculated that the whole of Mamma's plate and another suit of curtains for Nabby included would come at about 400 dollars. Mr. B. has 340 in his hands of Pappa's, about the sum that would buy all the things but Mamma's plate and Nabby's curtains; however, that makes not the least difference to Mr. Bowne, as he desires me to say he shall execute the commissions with great pleasure, and 'twill be no inconvenience to him to purchase the other articles, and I merely mentioned it as I did not know that you knew the real sum in Mr. Bowne's hands. 'Tis very lucky there is so direct an opportunity to Scarborough; we shall endeavor to send as many things as possible. Shopping at present is a prohibited pleasure to me, but as all the things can be better procured at wholesale stores, and my husband has both a great deal of taste and judgment in those things, and makes better bargains than I do, you will be no sufferer by the loss of my services in that, — and I can have anything sent to me to look at, and therefore 'tis quite as well as if I went for them. I don't mean you shall understand because I don't go shopping that I am confined to the house. On the contrary, I am much better than could be expected and hope with care to do very well. I shall go out very little until the middle or last of the winter, when I hope, if I continue well, to be most as smart as other people. My husband does not allow me to go into a shop. I laugh at him and tell him I don't believe but the health of his *purse* is *one-half* his concern — a fine excuse. Mrs. Bogert is in expectation of seeing Lucia Wadsworth when the General comes on. I have been confined to the house with a severe cold since Thursday, — Friday and Saturday was quite sick, and to-day feel unfit for anything almost but my bed. Adieu ; my best love to all the family. You mentioned nothing of the Cypher on the Plate : O. S. or B. — or your crest, or William's crest, if you can find them out, — I suppose we could here, — or what ? Mamma's I suppose will be S. only. I have a great mind to tell you what a saucy thing my husband said on your anxiety — that the bowls and edges of the spoons should not be sharp ; but I leave you to guess, or if you can't, perhaps William may help you to an explanation.

Adieu. Yours ever,

E. S. BOWNE.

Miss Octavia Southgate.

November 14, 1805.

Capt. Libby sails to-morrow ; we have got as many things as possible. There is not a piece of embossed Buff in New York, nor of plain either, there is not more than 2 pair alike, therefore I have done nothing about the trimmings. I fancy Boston is a better place for those things than New York. The most fashionable beds have draperies the same as my dimity window curtains. However, if you think best I will look farther, and perhaps there will be something new open in a week or two. There is but one barrel urn in the city. Mr. B. was two days in pursuit of one; he purchased this and sent it back: 'twas brown, and no plate on it except the nose. I can get you one like mine for $25. Let me know immediately respecting these things. Yesterday the Silversmith came for instructions respecting the plate, and bro't patterns for me to look at. I ordered a set of tea-things for Mamma the same as mine; I think them handsomer than any I see. The man is to send me some patterns to look at which he thinks are similar to your description. On the next page I will make a list of the goods and pieces copied from the bills.

1 piece Irish sheeting, 48 yards, at 5	$30.00
1 piece Irish sheeting, 55 yards, at 6/6	44.69
6 yards Fine Linen, at 7/6	5.62
12 Damask Napkins, at 8	12.00
1 piece fine Diaper 27 yards, at 5/6	18.56
2 Breakfast Cloths, at 14	3.50
1 plated Castor best kind,	12.00
1 plated Cake Basket silver rims	18.00
2 Pearl tea-pots, 2.25 ; 1 Trunk, 2.50	4.75
	$149.12

The sheeting is quite as cheap as mine, the fine I like very much and think it quite a bargain. The Diaper is not quite so cheap as mine, but it has risen ; the table-cloths are cheap, the linen is high I think. The Cake Basket is very cheap, $2 cheaper than mine, and rather handsomer I think. I could get no crimson marking, but send you a few skeins of cotton which I procured with much difficulty. The napkins are not the kind I wished, but there was none of those excepting at 2 places, and they were 18 / — 22 / a piece. I thought these pretty and would answer your purpose. I enclose the marking cotton and the key of the trunk. Adieu.

Yours ever,   E. S. Bowne.

P. S.   The bills are in Miranda's book in the trunk.

Jan. 14, 1806.

My dear Miranda :

Mr. Abbot is here from Brunswick and will take a letter for me to any of my friends. I should not have been surprised any more to have seen the cupola of the college itself walk into the room than I was to see Mr. Abbot, I could hardly believe my eyes ; but I could not but *know* him, as I know nobody like him : he always seems like a frightened bird — so hurried in his man-ner and conversation. How much he looked like some of Timothy Dexter's wooden men — at commencement last year; it came across my mind while he was sitting by me yesterday, — 'twas well I was alone, or I should

JAMES GORE KING

From a miniature in the possession of A. Gracie King, Esq.

have certainly laughed. Frederic,[1] I suppose, is at home, tho' Mr. A. could not tell me. John[2] and Charles King have some thought of going to Portland. I have told them they had better go some other time, as they will find Portland so dull and none of you in quite so good spirits. James is here and they return with him. You ask about Jane Watts — nobody sees her, she is entirely confined to her room. Doctor Burchea attends her now; her cough they think a little better, but she is not able to sleep at all without laudanum. I have no expectation she will recover, the family seem to have.

As to news — New York is not so gay as last Winter, few balls but a great many tea-parties. I believe I told you Mrs. Gillespie[3] has a daughter, and still more news. You never wrote me anything about the muslin for Arixene to work her a frock, 'tis so good an opportunity to send it that I have a great mind to get it notwithstanding. If you can, send the things I left to Louisa Davis in Boston. John and Charles would bring them on to me. Walter[4] will want the shirts as soon as the weather becomes warm. You say I have said nothing of Walter in any of my letters; he is so hearty and well I hardly thought of him when I wrote; he has not had a

[1] *Frederic Southgate*, her youngest brother.

[2] John, Charles, and James King, sons of Rufus King, Mrs. Bowne's cousins. James was at that time at Harvard College.

[3] Mrs. Gillespie (Amelia Denning). This daughter died when a very young girl of a putrid sore throat.

[4] Walter Bowne, Jr. Eldest child of Walter Bowne and Eliza Southgate.

day's sickness since I returned. I send him out walking frequently when 'tis so cold it quite makes the tears come; he trudges along with leading very well in the street, he never takes cold. He goes to bed at 6 o'clock, away in the room in the third story you used to sleep in, without fire or candle, and there he sleeps till Phœbe goes to bed to him. You know I am a great enemy to letting children sleep with a fire in the room; 'tis the universal practice here, and as long as I can avoid it I never mean to practice it; it subjects them to constant colds. They think I am very severe to suffer such a child to be put in the third story to sleep without a fire. I presume Aunt King and family are all well; they are going to have a fine *waffle* party on Tuesday. I wish you were here to go, for the boys want to have a fine frolic. Kitty Bayard[1] is to be married in April to Duncan Campbell; all engaged since Wolsey and Susan were married. Mary Watts[2] is engaged to the big Doctor Romaine, — that is quite a surprise to every one : this is rumor. And now I have written all the trifling, I come to what is nearer my heart. You are not half particular enough about Octavia. Does

[1] Kitty Bayard married Duncan Campbell. Her sister Susan had married Woolsey Rogers, December 1, 1807.

[2] Mary, oldest daughter of Robert Watts and his wife Lady Mary Alexander, married Dr. Romaine, who left her a widow after a few years of married life. At the age of seventy-three Mrs. Romaine married her first love, Peter Bertram Cruger, a widower with eight children. Miss Watts's engagement to Dr. Romaine was a surprise to her friends, who knew of her attachment to Mr. Cruger.

Isabella live in the same house she did when we were there? Has Octavia nobody with her to take care of her child? I am very glad to hear they are so cheerful. Pappa you say has been sick but is quite recovered. How is Mamma this winter, quite recovered her health?

Adieu. E. S. B.

Feb. 15.

And so I must hear of all the important events of the family from anybody who casually may have it in their power to communicate them. Horatio has a fine son, I hear, of which I am very glad; congratulate them for me — do they mean to call him the same name as their other little boy? I suppose you have heard from John and Charles King[1] since they have been in Boston. If you would send the little bundle for them to bring on I should be very glad, and I wish you to get me 3 pr. of Mr. Smith's little white worsted socks, such as I bo't for Walter, only two or three sizes larger, big enough for him next winter, — don't neglect it, for I wish for them very much. Let them be full large for a child 3 years

[1] John Alsop King, oldest son of Rufus King and his wife Mary Alsop. John A. King was twice governor of the State of New York. He married in 1810 Mary Ray. Charles King, the second son of Rufus King, for some time President of Columbia College, New York. He married twice: first, Miss Gracie, and for his second wife Miss Low, the daughter of his father's intimate friend Nicholas Low.

old. How are all the family? Octavia, I don't hear from anybody; you ought to write once a fortnight certainly. Poor Jane Watts is very low, confined to her bed, — I fear she will never go out again. Adieu; love to all. This is my second letter since I heard from you. I write more particularly that you may send those things by the boys.   **Yours ever,**   E. S. B.

To Mrs. Octavia Browne.

New York, March 30, 1806.

My Dear Mother :

I am most impatiently looking for Miranda and hoping, tho' I dare not place too much dependence on seeing my Father. I am better than when I wrote you before, tho' still subject to these faint turns. I have become more used to them and they don't alarm me. I ride frequently and take the air every fine day in some way or other. I have been free from a return of the nervous headache for a fortnight, till the night before last I had a return of the numbness and pain, tho' not so severe as the last. I have a very good appetite and look very fat and rosy, but really am very weak and languid. I don't know why I look so much better than I feel. Mary Murray is to be married a week from next Wednesday ; she is very desirous that Miranda should get here ; I really hope she may. Perhaps I may get courage enough to go myself if she comes in time, otherwise I don't believe I shall venture ; however, 'twill

CHARLES KING

From a miniature in the possession of his daughter, Mrs. Martin

depend upon my feelings at the time. I shall look out
the last of the week for Pappa and Miranda very seriously. I hope they are on their way now. Uncle's
oldest son, John Alsop, arrived here about a week since;
he seems a very fine young man, rather taller than his
Father, — he will be a second Uncle William, for he
does not appear to have half got his height. Charles
King has gone to Holland.   E. S. B.

    Mrs. Mary Southgate.

                      New York, April 27, 1806.

My Dear Mother :

Before you receive this my Father will be with you.
He says I need not fear any thing, that I am in a very
fair way of doing well; he will tell you all the particulars better than I could write. He got quite homesick,
we could not prevail on him to lengthen his visit or go
to the Springs and return here. I promised to let you
hear from me once a week how I got along. For the
last 3 days I have been finely, for me; the fore part of
the day I am often very faint — all the forenoon, but
generally better towards evening. 'Tis a great comfort
to me to have Miranda with me, as I am a great part of
the time unfit for anything. My head has been much
more clear and comfortable for the last few days than
for some time past. Tell Father there was a meeting
called last evening of the Federalists in the city, to

make some further remonstrances on the defenceless state of the Port of New York, occasioned by an accident that has set the whole City in an uproar. There are 3 British Frigates at the Hook, a few miles from the City, that fire upon all the vessels that come in or go out, and search them. They have sent several on to Halifax, and yesterday they fired in a most wanton manner upon a little coaster that was entering the harbor with only three men on board, and before they had time to come to as they were preparing to do, they fired again, and killed one of the men dead upon the spot, — he was brought up and the body exposed to view on one of the wharves, where several thousand people were collected to see it, — it put the City in great confusion, and this meeting was called in consequence — where Uncle made a very elegant speech. I am very sorry Father had not been here, it would have gratified him. 'Tis the first time he has spoken in public since his return to this Country. The British Consul had sent several boats of provisions down to the frigates — which as soon as 'twas known the Pilot-boats went after and brought them all back, — they were loaded upon carts and carried in procession thro' the streets to the poor house, attended by a prodigious mob — huzzaing, and the English and American colors fixed on the carts; they demanded the Commander of the frigate to be given up as a murderer by the British Consul, — he replied he had no power over him. It has made a prodigious noise in the City, as you may imagine. So much for Father;

— I shall expect to hear to-morrow when he got to Providence. Adieu, my dear Mother.

Ever your affectionate   E. S. BOWNE.

May 18.

By way of punishment, if it is any, I have denied myself the pleasure of answering your letter till I thought you would begin really to wish for a letter. However, I quite want to hear again, and as there is little hope of that until I answer yours, I'll e'en set about it at once. William Weeks told me he saw you in Portland the day before he left there. I wonder he did not tell you he was coming to New York. Mr. Isaac McLellan is here too from Portland. You did not write to me half particulars ; you said nothing about Arixene.

Sunday, May 25, 1806.

After a week has elapsed I resume my pen to finish my letter. I was expecting Mr. Isaac McLellan to call and let me know when he should return, as I intended writing by him, but he has left town without my knowing it. Now for news, which I suppose you are very anxious to hear. In the first place — Miss Laurelia Dashaway is married to Mr. Hawkes. On Saturday morning, 8 o'clock, Trinity Church was opened on purpose for the occasion ; something singular, as it would not be like Miss Laurelia. But what do you think —

Mr. Grellet has taken French leave of New York — sailed for France about a fortnight ago, without anybody's knowing their intention till they were gone. There are many conjectures upon the occasion not very favorable to the state of their finances. 'Tis said his friends were very averse to her going with him. If she had not, I suspect she must have sympathized with Madame Jerome Buonoparte and many other poor Madames that have founded their hopes on the fidelity of a Frenchman. Poor Mrs. Ogden has another little petticoated little John Murray — 4 daughters! — I am sorry it was not a boy. What should you think to see me come home without Mr. Bowne? I strongly fear he won't have it in his power to leave the office more than once in the Season ; if so, I would much prefer him to come for me in the Autumn. However, we have made no arrangements yet. Walter grows such a playful little rogue, he is always in mischief ; I am just leaving off his caps ; I want his hair to grow before his Grandmamma sees him ; he won't look so pretty without his caps. He creeps so much I find it impossible to keep him so nice as I used to. Poor Harriet Beam I think is going rapidly in a decline, she has been confined to her room 5 or 6 weeks. I have not seen the Wattses this some time ; they are gone to Passaic Falls with a little party, — Maria Laight, Mr. Delort, Robert Harney, etc. My love to all ; write me soon particularly. I hope soon to be with you. How is Sister Boyd's infant ?

Yours ever,   E. S. Bowne.

Miss Miranda Southgate.

New York, Nov. 8, 1806.

My Dear Octavia :

I am quite anxious to hear good news from you. Miranda has been in Jamaica this fortnight ; she has taken a frock and cap along with her to work for you ; I hope she will have it finished when she returns. Maria Denning is married, and William Duer has returned to New Orleans ; left her with her friends for the winter. Amelia was married to Mr. Gillespie in the spring ; lives at home yet.

Miss Pell was married last week to Robert Mac-Comb ; they are making a prodigious dash. I went to pay the bride's visit on Friday ; they had an elegant ball and supper in the evening, as it was the last day of seeing Company ; 7 brides-maids and 7 Bride-men, most superb dresses ; the bride's pearls cost 1,500 dollars ; they spend the winter in Charleston. Adieu ! Love to all friends, and tell your husband to write me immediately after this great event. I am looking forward to a happy summer spent among you. Best love to Isabella and family, Horatio and family. How is Robert Southgate junr.? That is as it ought to be. Pappa is pleased I dare say.

Yours ever,

Eliza S. Bowne.

My Dear Mother:

I find it quite in vain to wait for a letter from Miranda, and she has left me to chance and uncertainty to know whether she has ever arrived at Providence, but luckily, from constant enquiries, I have learnt she did arrive safe, and from some other accidental information, that she was to leave Boston last Thursday for home, with Judge Thatcher. I presume by this she is with you. As the Spring opens I begin to look forward to my Eastern visit. Octavia's boy is as beautiful as a cherub, I hear.

Saturday, 18th.

Miranda :

Mrs. Derby has returned from Philadelphia, and intends leaving here for Boston on Tuesday. She spent a long sociable day with me yesterday and I found it quite a treat; I have seen so little of her but in mix't parties that it hardly seems like a visit. She is almost worn out with dissipation, and I greatly fear her constitution has suffered an injury from this kind of life it will never recover. She has absolutely refused all invitations since her return, and means to rest for a few days while she remains here; she takes one of our *belles* on to Boston with her, — Miss Fairlie;[1] Miranda

---

[1] Miss Fairlee was the daughter of Major Fairlee of the British army, who was a noted wit. Many anecdotes are told of his odd sayings. One of them was, that being on his death-bed he was told by his physician to

knows her. Martha had a letter from Mrs. Sumner yesterday, where she mentions Miranda leaving there for home the Sunday before with Mr. and Mrs. Kinsman; I am really hurt at her unaccountable silence. I promised to tell her all the news and account of all the parties after she left me, but I was quite provoked at her not writing. Tell her, however, that there seems no end to the gaiety this Spring; it does not abate as yet at all. The day after she left me I paid the bride's visit to young Mrs. Murray; there was a prodigious crowd, a hundred and fifty at least, and many never sat down at all. Madame Moreau[1] wore a long black velvet dress with Pearl ornaments, looking elegantly. The next day I dined at Uncle Rufus King's with company; on Tuesday following, went to a ball at Mrs. Stevens';[2] next day, a ball at Miss Murray's, very pleasant; they very much regretted her not being here; she was intended to be one of the Bridesmaids; and the day after the last Assembly, as you may suppose, was completely tired dancing three nights in succession. Last Friday I was at a ball at the Watts's, and the week before at Miss Lyde's[3] to a

take yeast as medicine. "What for?" said the Major; "to make me rise?" Miss Fairlee married Cooper the actor.

[1] The wife of the French General Moreau. They came to the United States in 1805, but he returned to fight with the Allies, and was killed in 1813, some say by a bullet aimed by Napoleon himself.

[2] Mrs. Stevens was Miss Rachel Coxe, of Philadelphia, and had married Colonel Stevens, of Hoboken, New Jersey.

[3] Miss Lyde married Jonathan Ogden. Among her children were Mrs. Robert Goelet, Mrs. Dominick Lynch Lawrence, and Mrs. Joseph Ogden.

ball, and Mrs. Turnbull's to a monstrous tea-party.
Yesterday at Mrs. Morris'. On Monday next Aunt
King has a very large party. On Tuesday I go to Mrs.
Stoughton's, on Thursday to Mrs. Hopkins', and on
Friday dine at Mrs. Bogert's, and this evening to Mrs.
Henderson's to a *ball.* I think it will be one of the
most elegant we have had this winter. I wish Miranda
was here, — so much for Miranda. Adieu! I have
promised to go shopping with Mrs. Derby this morning
and 'tis growing late. I look forward with delight to
the approaching summer spent amidst all my family.

Give my affectionate regard to all.

Ever yours,   E. S. Bowne.

New York, Dec. 1, 1807.

You won't write a line I find without a punctual answer, letter for letter. Could not you make any allowance for domestic engagements, etc., etc., and write me
at present two for one, or were you afraid of the prece-
dent; I might claim as a right hereafter what I owed
merely to your indulgence. I have anxiously wished to
hear again from little William Brown, for, notwithstanding your flattering accounts of his returning health, I felt
so fully persuaded he would never recover that I could
not but think he would relapse again. How happy I
shall be to hear that my fears are groundless! If you
have not written again before this reaches you, lose no
time but write at once. I do not write to Octavia till I

know whether she is in Boston or Portland. You must make it a rule, Miranda, to write me once a fortnight whether I answer or not. Charles King will tell you all the news of the fashionable world. I have been in no parties yet. The Theatre is quite the rage. I have been several times, — you have no idea how much it is improved, entirely altered, — looks light and gay, — a perfect contrast to its former appearance. Cooper draws crowded houses every night — I have been much delighted. Mr. Wolsey Rogers' approaching nuptials seem anticipated as the opening of the winter campaign; of course the event is much talked of, not a mantua-maker in the city but will tell you some particulars of the bride's wardrobe, — length of her train, etc., etc. ; — a fine lady here, as Mustapha says, is estimated by the length of her tail. If it was not for using a most homely proverb, I would say "Every dog has his day." Here was our friend John Murray and his bride last winter, making all ring; this winter quietly settled in Nassau St., just what I call comfortable, (you have not seen this new play about *comfortable*.) Poor Sterlitz, who has no way to discover his taste or judgment but by finding fault with everything, seems quite in a *fuze* (is there such a word?) that Mr. Murray prefers his own comfort to dashing in high style. I suppose, Mrs. B. begins to feel all the palpitations and trepidations of a doating anxious mother in introducing her favorite daughter to the world. The next winter is the all-important era for the exhibition. Miss A., in my opinion, will make a

little coquette — the bud seems expanding even now, —
that extreme simplicity, which her mother encouraged
by always talking of it before her, as if she was too
young to understand, is now changing for an affectation
of simplicity.   I hope she will correct it ; time will convince her that simplicity is only charming in inexperienced youth, or rather the kind of simplicity which
she possesses.   There *is* a simplicity which gives a soft-
ness, a *tone* (as a painter would say) to the whole character, but it springs uncontaminated from the guileless
purity of the mind ; all affectation of this serves but
as a tattered veil thro' which you constantly penetrate
to the original deformity —   Where have I rambled ?
Poor Mrs. Greene is dangerously ill, her friends have
little hope of her recovery.   On Saturday she was not
expected to live the day, — bled several quarts at the
lungs ; she is a favorite with all who know her, a most
valuable woman.   On business : — Mamma told me
something about getting muslin for Arixene — a frock to
work, but I have forgotten whether she afterwards told
me to get it or not.   I can get very pretty for 2 dollars
or 2 1-2 ; let me know.   Tell Octavia I received the
little hat which Mr. Browne bo't for me in Boston, and
shall send the little *tub* and the rest of the money, as
soon as I know she is in Boston.   Fashions : — Ladies
wear fawn-colored coats and bonnets of the same
trimmed with velvet trimming, same color with lappets,
cape and inner waistcoat.   If I could find an opportunity I should send you a bonnet and Mamma a cap.

Adieu, — tell Arixene to write to me. James King writes to Charles King he liked Arixene best of all the Cousins.

To Miss Miranda Southgate.

New York, Dec. 13, 1807.

I have been waiting some time to hear you were in Boston, but as I have not heard from any of the family for some weeks I shall write you and direct to Portland. I am rejoiced to hear that little William continues to recover fast, for Mrs. Derby writes me still later than Miranda that he is almost recovered. How happy you must feel! None but those who have suffered the anxiety can conceive the happiness of such a change. I don't hear half often enough from you. Miranda writes but seldom. Charles King told me last evening, in his last letter from her she says she is going to spend part of the winter in Boston with you, — from that I conclude you intend going to housekeeping before Spring. I have been making a plan for you to make me a visit next Spring. I think there can be no objection to it ; your husband can make arrangements to leave Boston for a month or a few weeks, I am sure. The accommodations in the stage to Providence are so good, you can go in half a day — take passage in a Packet and be in New York in three days with ease. You can either bring William with you, which I should wish you to, or leave him if you prefer it. Indeed I can see no objection to the plan. Your friends in New York have made particular enquiries respecting you. Mary Murray says you have quite given her up, that she has not received a line from you for some time — I don't remember how long. I believe I told you Mrs. Ogden had lost her youngest child, about 5 months old. Harriet Beam, whom I believe you knew, died last week, — melancholy, so young. Mrs. Derby writes me her Father is still far from strong and firm, tho' much better ; very probable his constitution will never entirely recover this shock. I am much obliged to Mr. Browne for purchasing the little hat for Walter. It was not the kind I meant, however, — those here are worn only by girls, square crowns altogether for boys. Give my best love to Horatio and Nabby, Isabella and husband, Arixene — I want to send her a pattern·to work a frock in ; I have a very pretty one, with but little work on. Adieu ; write me very particularly about William. E. S. BOWNE.

To Mrs. Wm. Browne (Octavia Southgate).

New York, Jan. 13, 1808.

I have been in daily expectation of hearing farther from you, my dear Miranda. I received a letter from Octavia by the same mail that brought me yours, informing me of the melancholy change in their prospects, which I answered immediately and used every argument I thought could console her at such a time. Her firmness and resolution in relating the particulars, her reasoning on the subject, displayed the real superiority of her mind. She has had severe trials ; the danger of her child, and now this stroke ; I tremble when I think with how much less firmness I should probably have acted in the same trials. I am extremely anxious to hear all the particulars of their failure, how Mr. Browne bears it, where they will spend their winter. I wish with all my heart Octavia and her child would come and stay with me until Mr. Browne could arrange his affairs a little. But I suppose 'twould be in vain to urge her to leave her husband at this time. You mention that you were in hopes Papa would secure Octavia's furniture for her. I wish you would write me particularly if he did. Octavia writes me he attached all the personal property he knew of at the time. Pappa too I fear will be quite a sufferer by their failure. I hear Webster is gone, — he, I think, had money of my Father's. Mr. Bowne has always thought he played rather a hazardous game in letting out money in that way. I hope he is not materially injured, — he will, at any rate, have the consolation to know that the education of his children is principally accomplished ; he will always have enough to live with comfort and ease, and as to leaving a great deal, I think 'tis very immaterial. I am glad to find his stock here has produced a very good dividend this month. I hope this won't depress his spirits any, — old people feel the loss of property much more than younger ones. However, Papa's is nothing to mention at these times, as he is not in debt, has a good farm, and will always have all the comforts of life; indeed, I think 'twill have a good effect. He has always been determined on leaving such a sum untouched, and from that darling object has deprived himself of the comfort of a comfortable house for many years past. Accident has interfered with the fulfilment of his plan; he will now enjoy what he has left without thinking of leaving just so much; his children are, or soon will be grown up, and he ought to have no other care but to enjoy what he has dearly earned, now in his old age. I am sure all his children most heartily wish it, if he should not leave a farthing for them. Old Mr. Codwise has failed, a dreadful thing for so old a man. Mr. Macomb [Ann and Robert's father] is gone too; all the Franklins too, and a great many others I do not now recollect. Adieu; write me immediately and tell me every particular. My love to Arixene; is she at Miss Martin's, for I have never heard?

E. S. BOWNE.

Miss Miranda Southgate.

Boston, December 21, 1808.

My best Friends:

In consequence of a letter from Mr. Bowne, received this day, I have to inform you that instead of proceeding to Scarborough, my next journey is to New York. He writes me that by the advice of Mr. King they have concluded it will be best for Eliza to go to Charleston, South Carolina, in order to avoid the severity of our winter; that he is under the necessity of remaining in

New York till February himself, and that he wishes me to return and go on with Eliza and Octavia as soon as I can. As I have nothing of consequence to prevent me, I shall leave this in a day or two for New York, and shall be fully satisfied if I can render them the least service by my attentions. With sentiments of the highest esteem and regard,

I am your·obedient servant   W. Browne.

To Mr. and Mrs. Southgate.

New York, Dec. 27, 1808.

You are anxious, my Dear Mother, to hear from my own hand how I am. Octavia has told you all my complaints: my cough is extremely obstinate, I have occasionally a little fever, tho' quite irregular and sometimes a week without any. I have a new Physician to attend me; he is a Frenchman of great celebrity, particularly in Pulmonary complaints, and has been wonderfully successful in the cure of coughs; he keeps me on a milk diet, but allows me to eat eggs and oysters. He does not give any opiates; Paregoric and Laudanum he entirely disapproves of; he gives no medicine but a decoction of Roots and Flowers; — the *Iceland Moss* or *Lichen* made in a tea he gives a great deal of, and for cough I take a white Pectoral lotion he calls it, made principally of White Almonds, Gum Arabic, Gum Tragacanth (or something like it), the Syrup of Muskmelon seeds. He thinks I am much better already. I have no pain at all, and have not had any. My cough seems to be all my disorder. He thinks he can cure that; indeed he speaks with perfect confidence, and says he has no doubt as soon as I get to warmer weather, my cough will soon leave me. Mr. Browne got here last night, and we shall probably sail by Sunday at farthest. Octavia will write particularly. You will hear from me, my Dear Mother, often, — at present my mind seems so occupied; leaving my children, preparing to go, and making arrangements to shut up my house. 'Tis quite a trial to leave my little ones; I leave them at their Grandmother's. My little Mary[1] has a wet-nurse; she is a fine, lively child, and thrives fast. Adieu, my Dear Mother; I did not think I could have written half as much; love to all my friends.

ELIZA S. BOWNE.

Charleston, South Carolina, Jan. 1, 1809.

Our most esteemed Friends :

We have now been in the City a week. We find that Eliza has gained a little strength since she arrived, and that her cough is not quite so distressing as before we left New York. She complains of no pain, but her fever and night sweats continue to trouble her every other day and night, as was the case before. She can walk about her room with ease; and she rides when the weather is fine, which she is much pleased with, and no doubt it is of great service to her. The streets are entirely of sand, as smooth as possible, no pavements, not

1 Mrs. John Lawrence.

a stone to be seen, which renders it very easy riding for her. It is as warm as our first of May, (if not the middle,) and when the weather is fair, the air is clear, very mild and refreshing. The change is so great between this and New York that I cannot help thinking it must have a great and good effect on Eliza. I find as to myself that my cough is done away entirely, and I had a little of it most all the time at home in winter. Octavia has certainly grown fat, and our little Frederic is very well indeed. Eliza eats hominy, rice and milk, eggs and oysters cooked in various ways, vegetables too, which we find in great perfection here; fruit is plenty of almost every description. The oranges raised here are not sweet but are very large. Their olives, grapes, and figs are excellent. Their meats and fish are not so good as ours. Their Poultry is fine; a great plenty of Venison, wild ducks, and small sea-fowl; green peas we shall have in about a month; so that, beside the change of climate, we have many of the luxuries of a Northern summer. Uncle King gave us letters to Gen. C. C. Pinckney and his brother Major Thomas Pinckney, — both of them being out of town at their plantation; their sister, Mrs. Hovey, received the letters and has been very attentive and kind to us all. She is a widow, about 55 I should judge, of the first respectability, and appears a very pleasant, amiable and cheerful old lady. She sends some nice things to Eliza almost every day. Her daughters, Mrs. Rutledge, two Miss Pinckneys (daughters of the General), Mrs. Gilchrist and daughter, Mr.

and Mrs. Mannigault, Mrs. Middleton, Mr. and Mrs.
Izard,[1] Mr. and Mrs. Dessault and Mr. Heyward make
an extensive acquaintance for us. They all seem very
kind and hospitable to us, plain and open in their manners, and yet the most genteel and easy. Eliza has
seen only Mrs. Hovey, Mrs. Rutledge, and the two
Miss Pinckneys, but she thinks in a few days to be able
to receive short visits from a few of her friends, and
even thinks it may be of consequence to enliven her.
She rides whenever the weather is fine, and is very much
pleased with the appearance of everything growing in
the gardens here so like our June. We have had one
visit from a Physician only ; he thinks taking a little
blood from her would be of service, but she has not yet
consented. He approved of her diet and of the Iceland
Moss tea which was recommended at New York, and
which is said here to have had a great effect in removing complaints of the cough. Mrs. Mannigault told us
yesterday she found immediate relief from it after she
had been sick a long time. We expect Mr. Bowne in
the course of a fortnight, and then I expect to return

[1] Ralph Izard and his wife, the granddaughter of Etienne de Lanci, a
Huguenot nobleman who came to this country in 1686. Mr. Izard had
been appointed Commissioner from Congress to the grand-duchy of
Tuscany, and had performed other important diplomatic services. He
was one of the first United States senators from South Carolina. Mrs.
Mannigault's husband was the grandson of Mr. and Mrs. Izard. She was
related to the Misses Watts of New York, and for their sake was particularly attentive and kind to their friend Mrs. Bowne. Mr. and Mrs. Heyward were the parents of the celebrated beauty Miss Elizabeth Heyward,
who married James Hamilton.

toward Scarborough immediately. We hope to hear from you in a few days ; not a word have we yet from New York since we arrived. Our darling boy we think we see every day playing about us, without thinking who admires him at the distance of 1100 miles.

Our best wishes attend you always.

Affectionately, W. Browne.

To Mr. and Mrs. Southgate.

Charleston, Jan. 28, 1809.

Dear Caroline, I send by Capt. Crowel a little pair of shoes for Mary, a little Cuckoo toy for Walter, and a tumbler of Orange Marmalade for Mother. I have had only one letter from New York since I have been here, and that from Mary Perkins, not one line from my husband. I can tell you nothing flattering of my health : I am very miserable ; at present I have a kind of intermittent Fever ; this afternoon I shall take an emetic, and hope a good effect. How are my dear little ones ? — I hope not too troublesome. Octavia is in fine health and grows quite fat for her. Frederic has been unusually troublesome. My dear little Walter ! — I hardly trust myself to think of them, — precious children — how they bind me to life ! Adieu. I have a bad headache and low-spirited to-day. Eliza.

Caroline Bowne (with 2 small parcels),
No. 288 Pearl Street,
Blazing Star. New York.

This appears to be the last letter written by Mrs. Bowne. (M. K. L.)

From Mrs. William Browne to Mrs. King.

Charleston, February 2, 1809.

I have been waiting day after day, my Dear Aunt, in the hope of having something pleasant to communicate to you, but I do very much fear I shall now have nothing, if ever, to say about our Dear Eliza but will give you pain. I sat down to write to you without knowing what to say. I have been so in the habit of dissembling lately that I can hardly throw it off, for when I write my Father and Mother everything is so glossed over, 'tis impossible to come at the truth. You know not how I am affected, my Dear Aunt. I fear I am doing wrong in deceiving them, for it is my firm opinion she never will be well. Do advise me, tell me what I ought to do. I think to you I may say the truth — I think she has been growing sicker every hour since she left New York. Her voyage had a singular effect upon her: she suffered but little from seasickness, but every bad symptom she had before seemed increased ; she coughed a great deal and very hard, her fever and night sweats were excessive. You may imagine she was much weakened ; but I hoped this was a temporary thing, and a few days of quiet and of rest would restore her ; but instead of that, directly after our arrival a sort of intermittent fever took place, she had a regular chill and fever every day, she lost her strength very much, no appetite at all. This last four or five days her disorder wears another appearance. 'Tis now Thursday. On Sunday Dr. Irvine ordered her to take Quashy in order

to prevent a chill; she took it according to his direction
— it brought on her fever at 1 o'clock in the morning,
and it never left her till 12 o'clock at night, it absolutely raged all day. Since then she has had no night
sweats, no chill, but her cough and fever very much increased. Her nerves are extremely disordered; such a
tremor that to-day she cannot feed herself at all. She
is so weak and exhausted that she cannot walk alone.
'Tis now 11 o'clock — I am sitting by her side, and she
is still coughing and in such a hot fever she can bear
nothing to touch her. I have not asked her Physician's
opinion concerning her; 'tis unnecessary I feel, I know
what it must be. Yet is it not strange she keeps up
her spirits? She is looking forward with the greatest
anxiety to warm weather. God grant it may not be
too late! Dr. Irvine was the Physician Mrs. Hovey
recommended; he is indisposed and has left his patients
in the care of Dr. Barrow. The exchange has pleased
us very much, for Dr. Barrow is considered quite as
skilful, and is extremely kind and fatherly in his manners, indeed he reminds us so strongly of our Dear
Father that we already love him very much.

February 3.

Poor Eliza had a most distressing night last night. She
coughed so long that she was entirely exhausted; her
fever was very high, and she has scarcely spoken a loud
word to-day. Her nerves are in a dreadful state. I in-

quired of Dr. Barrow what he thought of her situation ;
he says he can say nothing encouraging. He said the
disorder had taken great hold upon her, and had shat-
tered her nerves in a terrible manner. He very much
fears a nervous fever, — that her pulse was very bad, as
nearly as he could count up to 150. Is it not very evi-
dent from his being so candid, my Dear Aunt, that he
has but little or no hope of her recovery ? And yet so
strongly do I sympathize in every feeling of hers, that
seeing her easier and more comfortable this evening
has renewed my hopes and put me quite in spirits. She
has been much better this afternoon and evening, less
fever, less tremor upon her nerves, and since she has
been in bed has had no bad coughing spell. The mail
went to the Northward to-day. I have so little time to
write that I have missed it. I will let you know to-
morrow how she is, and the next day is post-day again.
I know what a kind interest you and my uncle take
in our dear Eliza, and I know I cannot be too minute.
Our friends here are kinder than I can express to you.
It seems sometimes as though we were among our own
relations. They think of every little thing for Eliza's
comfort and convenience that I could myself.

Monday, February 6.

This morning Eliza was better, my Dear Aunt, than
she has been for a week past. Her voice has returned
and she appears stronger in every respect. Yesterday

and last night she had a little fever, this morning is delightful and she is going to ride. You shall hear again from us before long. I know Mrs. Bogert will need no apology, I am sure, for my not writing. The repetition of such symptoms are distressing to me beyond expression.   Your affectionate niece   O. S. BROWNE.

To Mrs. Bowne.

New York, Feb'y 4, 1809.

Your letter, my love, of the 13th and 14th has comforted me. You must keep up your spirits; you will do well, Dr. Bergere says ; attacks similar to yours are not of the dangerous kind that some think ; he approves of your taking the Lychen again. I have sent a bundle from Mr. King by Capt. Slocum, who sails to-morrow. I am distressed I cannot go with him, but so it is. It is next to impossible I should leave here till about the 25th of this month. Mr. Jenkins, my assistant, is absent, and I cannot leave the office until he returns without relinquishing it altogether, and I have most of my houses to let this month, those I have lately built included, and which are not finished, but I am determined to leave here in all this month. I hope you have a comfortable place now ; what abominable lodgings the first were ! Don't mind the expense : get everything and do everything you like, we can afford it. I wish my presence in this place could as well be dispensed with, but so it is. I think it right you should have a Physician.   I will bring the things you mention; our children are well.   Ever,   WALTER BOWNE.

The Ship — General Eaton — has not yet arrived, I will write to Mr. Brown by this vessel if I have time ; if not, by mail on Monday or Tuesday.

(With a bundle of Lychen for E. S. B.)

The following letter from Mr. Rufus King to his nephew Horatio Southgate, will show how much alarm was felt about Mrs. Bowne's health.

Dear Sir :   New York, February 9, 1809.

I have to beg your excuse that I have so long delayed my answer to your letter written I believe in November. The Plants were a long time on their way, and did not arrive till Christmas, when we had a few days of mild weather, which enabled us to put them in the ground. Mr. Mars is entitled to credit for the manner and care with which the Plants were packed, and altho' they were much longer out of the ground than they sh^d have been, I am in hopes that many of them were saved. Inclosed I send you a Post-note (payable to your order) on the Boston Branch Bank for 47 dollars, being the amount of Mars's account, and I beg you to accept my acknowledgments for the trouble you have given yourself in this Business.   Should there be an opportunity direct from Portland to N. York in the Spring, any time in Ap^l or May would do (for that is the true season, even on to the middle of June, to remove evergreens), I wish Mars to send me a few more spruces, one moderate sized Box, together with some of the small Evergreen shrubs found in the woods and pastures, and which I remember abounded in the Pasture of Knight's Farm, and which we called laurel, or sheep poison. Any other small plants may be added to fill up the Box.

We yesterday heard from Mrs. Bowne, who had recovered from the fatigue of her voyage, and thought herself something better. I am in hopes that the soft weather of an early spring will do more for her than medicine could have effected in the rude weather of our winter and spring. I ought not to conceal from you, tho' I think you sh^d not unnecessarily increase the anxiety of your mother, that I am not free from apprehensions regarding your Sister's complaint; it is so flattering and insidious, that I do not place the same Reliance upon favorable Reports w^h in any other case I sh^d be inclined to do. I by no means think that she has no chance of recovery. On the contrary, I have the satisfaction to believe and expect that she will regain her accustomed good health. Mrs. Browne's being with her is a very important circumstance in a case in which good nursing and careful attention is of so much consequence.

With sincere Regards, I remain, Dr Sir,

Y^r obliged serv't,   Rufus King.

Horatio Southgate, Esqr., Portland, Maine.

Charleston, February 21, 1809.

I will permit no one but myself to transmit to you the dreadful intelligence this letter will convey to you, my dear Parents. A good and merciful God will not forsake you at this awful moment. Our dear Eliza is freed from her earthly sufferings and I humbly trust is now a blessed spirit in Heaven! I offer you no consolation; I commit you into the hands of a Good God, who has supported me when my strength failed me. She had her senses at intervals for the few days last of her illness. She spoke of her approaching change with great composure, said she had thought much of it, that she trusted in God for future happiness with great satisfaction and confidence; wished her time might come speedily that she might be relieved from the pain of seeing her distressed friends. She suffered with wonderful patience; never murmured. At the very last she looked the satisfaction she had not the power to speak. At 2 o'clock yesterday afternoon was this most afflicting scene. Octavia had great fortitude to sit by her when she could speak only with her eyes. She knew us, and listened with apparent satisfaction to a prayer I read only an hour before the sad moment. It was a day of trial with us most severe.

With much affection and regard to all,

W. BROWNE.

Poor Mr. Bowne has not arrived.

To Mr. & Mrs. Southgate.

Charleston, March 12, 1809.

I hope, my dear Miranda, this will be the last letter you will receive from me at Charleston. Poor Mr. Bowne arrived here on Thursday. Not a word had he heard, and owing to his having left New York he had not received a single very alarming letter. He was entirely unprepared for the shock which awaited him ; never did I pity any one so. He is indeed borne down with the weight of his grief. But the violence I dreaded I see nothing of. There is no judging from the effect little troubles have upon people, how they will bear great ones. I know it by myself — I see it in him. He is more composed to-day, and we are making arrangements to get away. He is much gratified that we waited here for him, which we had some doubt about on account of the great expense in these houses. The Minerva, a very fine Packet, arrived from New York yesterday. We shall return in her. She will go in the course of a week or ten days. What a melancholy voyage ! But yet I will not think so. I am going to my dear father and mother, my kind sisters, — indeed, 'tis a delightful thought.

Your sister,

O. Browne.

Among the letters which were so carefully preserved by her daughter, Mrs. Lawrence, was found the following extract from a daily paper : —

Died at Charleston, S. C., on the 19th ult., Mrs. Walter Bowne, consort of Walter Bowne, Esq., of New York, and daughter of the Hon. Robert Southgate, of Scarborough, Maine, aged 25 years. The Bereaved Husband and infant children, the afflicted parents, Brethren and sisters, and the numerous respectable friends and acquaintances by whom she was so justly respected and beloved for her talents and virtues, will deeply mourn this early signal triumph of the King of Terrors. But they will not " sorrow as those without hope." Her immortal spirit, liberated from the body, is, we trust, already admitted to a clear and perfect, an immediate and positive, a soul-transforming and eternal vision of God and the Redeemer. Why the most endearing ties of nature should be dissolved almost as soon as formed, why the dreadful law of mortality should be executed on the most worthy and dearest objects of conjugal, parental, and social love, in the moment of sanguine expectation of reciprocal enjoyment, is among the dark and mysterious questions in the book of Providence. The ways of God are inscrutable to man, " clouds and darkness are round about him, yet righteousness and judgment are the habitation of his throne." All afflictive events are readily resolved into the wisdom of God. To his sovereign will, reason and religion, duty and interest require us to bow with reverence. What a dark and gloomy veil is spread by the early death of our friends over our earthly enjoyments ! How tenderly are we hereby admonished not to expect satisfaction in this empty, fluctuating, and transitory state ! How strongly urged to place our affections on things above, to secure an immediate interest in those sublime and durable pleasures which flow from the service and favor of God and the prospect of complete and endless felicity in His presence.

Inscription on the monument in Archdale Church-yard, in Archdale Street, Charleston, S. C. : —

SACRED

TO THE MEMORY OF

ELIZA S. BOWNE

Wife of Walter Bowne of New York,
Daughter of Robert Southgate Esqr.,
of Scarborough, District of Maine,
who departed this life on the 19th
day of February, 1809, aged 25 years.

Women in America

FROM COLONIAL TIMES TO THE 20TH CENTURY

An Arno Press Collection

Andrews, John B. and W. D. P. Bliss. **History of Women in Trade Unions** (*Report on Conditions of Woman and Child Wage-Earners in the United States,* Vol. X; 61st Congress, 2nd Session, Senate Document No. 645). 1911

Anthony, Susan B. **An Account of the Proceedings on the Trial of Susan B. Anthony, on the Charge of Illegal Voting at the Presidential Election in November, 1872,** and on the Trial of Beverly W. Jones, Edwin T. Marsh and William B. Hall, the Inspectors of Election by Whom her Vote was Received. 1874

The Autobiography of a Happy Woman. 1915

Ayer, Harriet Hubbard. **Harriet Hubbard Ayer's Book:** A Complete and Authentic Treatise on the Laws of Health and Beauty. 1902

Barrett, Kate Waller. **Some Practical Suggestions on the Conduct of a Rescue Home.** *Including* **Life of Dr. Kate Waller Barrett** (Reprinted from *Fifty Years' Work With Girls* by Otto Wilson). [1903]

Bates, Mrs. D. B. **Incidents on Land and Water;** Or, Four Years on the Pacific Coast. 1858

Blumenthal, Walter Hart. **Women Camp Followers of the American Revolution.** 1952

Boothe, Viva B., editor. **Women in the Modern World** (*The Annals of the American Academy of Political and Social Science,* Vol. CXLIII, May 1929). 1929

Bowne, Eliza Southgate. **A Girl's Life Eighty Years Ago:** Selections from the Letters of Eliza Southgate Bowne. 1888

Brooks, Geraldine. **Dames and Daughters of Colonial Days.** 1900

Carola Woerishoffer: Her Life and Work. 1912

Clement, J[esse], editor. **Noble Deeds of American Women;** With Biographical Sketches of Some of the More Prominent. 1851

Crow, Martha Foote. **The American Country Girl.** 1915

De Leon, T[homas] C. **Belles, Beaux and Brains of the 60's.** 1909

de Wolfe, Elsie (Lady Mendl). **After All.** 1935

Dix, Dorothy (Elizabeth Meriwether Gilmer). **How to Win and Hold a Husband.** 1939

Donovan, Frances R. **The Saleslady.** 1929

Donovan, Frances R. **The Schoolma'am.** 1938

Donovan, Frances R. **The Woman Who Waits.** 1920

Eagle, Mary Kavanaugh Oldham, editor. **The Congress of Women,** Held in the Woman's Building, World's Columbian Exposition, Chicago, U.S.A., 1893. 1894

Ellet, Elizabeth F. **The Eminent and Heroic Women of America.** 1873

Ellis, Anne. **The Life of an Ordinary Woman.** 1929

[Farrar, Eliza W. R.] **The Young Lady's Friend.** By a Lady. 1836

Filene, Catherine, editor. **Careers for Women.** 1920

Finley, Ruth E. **The Lady of Godey's:** Sarah Josepha Hale. 1931 **Fragments of Autobiography.** 1974

Frost, John. **Pioneer Mothers of the West;** Or, Daring and Heroic Deeds of American Women. 1869

[Gilman], Charlotte Perkins Stetson. **In This Our World.** 1899

Goldberg, Jacob A. and Rosamond W. Goldberg. **Girls on the City Streets:** A Study of 1400 Cases of Rape. 1935

Grace H. Dodge: Her Life and Work. 1974

Greenbie, Marjorie Barstow. **My Dear Lady:** The Story of Anna Ella Carroll, the "Great Unrecognized Member of Lincoln's Cabinet." 1940

Hourwich, Andria Taylor and Gladys L. Palmer, editors. **I Am a Woman Worker:** A Scrapbook of Autobiographies. 1936

Howe, M[ark] A. De Wolfe. **Memories of a Hostess:** A Chronicle of Friendships Drawn Chiefly from the Diaries of Mrs. James T. Fields. 1922

Irwin, Inez Haynes. **Angels and Amazons:** A Hundred Years of American Women. 1934

Laughlin, Clara E. **The Work-a-Day Girl:** A Study of Some Present-Day Conditions. 1913

Lewis, Dio. **Our Girls.** 1871

Liberating the Home. 1974

Livermore, Mary A. **The Story of My Life; Or,** The Sunshine and Shadow of Seventy Years . . . To Which is Added Six of Her Most Popular Lectures. 1899

Lives to Remember. 1974

Lobsenz, Johanna. **The Older Woman in Industry.** 1929

MacLean, Annie Marion. **Wage-Earning Women.** 1910

Meginness, John F. **Biography of Frances Slocum, the Lost Sister of Wyoming:** A Complete Narrative of her Captivity of Wanderings Among the Indians. 1891

Nathan, Maud. **Once Upon a Time and Today.** 1933

[Packard, Elizabeth Parsons Ware]. **Great Disclosure of Spiritual Wickedness!!** In High Places. With an Appeal to the Government to Protect the Inalienable Rights of Married Women. 1865

Parsons, Alice Beal. **Woman's Dilemma.** 1926

Parton, James, et al. **Eminent Women of the Age:** Being Narratives of the Lives and Deeds of the Most Prominent Women of the Present Generation. 1869

Paton, Lucy Allen. **Elizabeth Cary Agassiz:** A Biography. 1919

Rayne, M[artha] L[ouise]. **What Can a Woman Do; Or,** Her Position in the Business and Literary World. 1893

Richmond, Mary E. and Fred S. Hall. **A Study of Nine Hundred and Eighty-Five Widows Known to Certain Charity Organization Societies in 1910.** 1913

Ross, Ishbel. **Ladies of the Press:** The Story of Women in Journalism by an Insider. 1936

Sex and Equality. 1974

Snyder, Charles McCool. **Dr. Mary Walker:** The Little Lady in Pants. 1962

Stow, Mrs. J. W. **Probate Confiscation:** Unjust Laws Which Govern Woman. 1878

Sumner, Helen L. **History of Women in Industry in the United**

States (*Report on Conditions of Woman and Child Wage-Earners in the United States,* Vol. IX; 61st Congress, 2nd Session, Senate Document No. 645). 1910

[Vorse, Mary H.] **Autobiography of an Elderly Woman.** 1911

Washburn, Charles. **Come into My Parlor:** A Biography of the Aristocratic Everleigh Sisters of Chicago. 1936

Women of Lowell. 1974

Woolson, Abba Gould. **Dress-Reform:** A Series of Lectures Delivered in Boston on Dress as it Affects the Health of Women. 1874

Working Girls of Cincinnati. 1974